COME INTO MY FATHER'S TEEPEE

THE HEAVENLY FAMILY

LOCKLEY C. BREMNER

Illustrated by Christina Y Mcnabb

ISBN: 979-8-89216-014-8 (Paperback)

Library of Congress Control Number: 2024912642

BookmarcAlliance
California, USA
www.bookmarcalliance.com

TABLE OF CONTENTS

Forward v

Introduction vii

Chapter 1   The Sovereign Sons Of Yhwh......................1

Chapter 2   The Emergence Of Nation/City States......17

Chapter 3   The Beginning Of The Family Of God......40

Chapter 4   The Institutionalized Enslavement
             Conspiracy...55

Chapter 5   The Heavenly Family (The Agapeo)...........65

Chapter 6   From The Church To The Oikos................ 77

Chapter 7   The Spiritual Realm 94

Chapter 8   The Battle For Planet Earth....................100

Chapter 9   Transference Of Authority......................108

Chapter 10   A New Reformation 118

Chapter 11   The Ministry Of Jesus Christ..................133

Chapter 12   What Is God's Name?.............................144

Chapter 13   Spiritual Warfare....................................168

Chapter 14   "The Sign Of The Son Of Man".............178

Sources Consulted 189

FORWARD

SOME YEARS AGO, I attended brother Lockley's yearly "Camp Meetings" he held many miles back in the wilderness on the Flathead reservation. From many parts of the country, people gathered and camped beside a rushing stream for three days like one big family. Throughout this time, we worshipped in Native American fashion, making "Grand entries", beating drums and dancing. In the evening we sat around camp fires extolling the wonders of God. It was in this wilderness setting where I began to discover the deeply wounded cry within the hearts of the "Native American." Contrary to European thought, the Native people were not savages, but a culture that was deeply family oriented and honoring the family generations beginning with the patriarch.

In light of this forward, and as you begin reading this book; you will discover a totally new meaning of biblical understanding, all the way from Genesis 1, to Revelation 22.

Brother Lockley, is not only recognized to be a spiritual warrior over the Blackfoot nation, but also recognized by many others across the US and Canada. He will lead you through many deep spiritual revelations that can only be found in the store house of the long forgotten Native culture. Within these writings He will at times expound on various Native beliefs and traditions that may not always be understood through our structured minds of the Americanized church.

Do not allow this to mar your thinking—keep reading! You will find this to be a revolutionary message, a message that will liberate you.

One of the keys in his message is our often undiscovered, sovereign and personal relationship with YHWH, and this, without the baggage and mindset of our cultural church structure. This message has personally lifted me above the clouds where I was able to connect with the heart of YHWH in an unprecedented level.

It is here, where we can learn and discover some of the treasures hidden away within the hearts of our Native American brothers. His mission was to relate to me, how, from his culture he relates to YHWH, and how YHWH relates to him. For us White people, this is often a stretch to think in terms of our Native brothers.

Consequently, for some, this book will be controversial; some may not even accept the message. But we also tend to forget, few men walked this earth who were more controversial then Jesus Himself. His controversy continues today; through men whose message at times challenges the broad and accepted paths of the western mindset—even so, each of us still have the liberty of choice. May YHWH be glorified.

Ben Girod
Founder of Anabaptist Connections
www.anabaptistconnections.org

INTRODUCTION

"The voice of one crying in the wilderness;
Prepare the way of the Lord [YHWH];
Make straight in the desert a highway for our God."
(Isaiah 40:3)

WE ARE LIVING IN times of change. We are witnessing a revolution in the world that is overturning establishment entrenchment and a new era of enlightenment is dawning. a new wave is here. People are becoming aware of the corruption of the established order and are demanding realignment. The same thing is happening in the spiritual realm where seekers are awakening to the fact that the same old religiosity over and over again is not working. Never before in history have so many people been so hungry for the next move of God. People are grasping for something new and meaningful, yet more often than not, they are handed empty illusions. It's time for the new wave.

In this writing, I upset the money tables of the established religious order and present a new perspective that will stimulate longing hearts of hungry seekers. In this writing I present a new model, the vision of **the Heavenly Family**, God's heart and plans from the beginning. I expose mystery Babylon, and reveal the true identity of God. I uncover how the nations of the earth are an antithesis of the Kingdom of God and are in fact making war against their Creator. Believe me, this treatise is *not* Morgan Freeman's description of god.

My journey began many years ago on the Blackfeet Indian Reservation in Montana. I admit that my upbringing was socially isolated, and innocent. As far as a world view is concerned, I didn't have a clue. As a boy, I spent most of my time riding my horse, picking berries and playing with my dog. Today, as I look around the world and our country, I see that people in the world don't have a clue either. People's world views are fairly small, and the Enemy we are up against is a master strategist whose conspiracies has been unfolding since the beginning. As I see it, the psyche of humanity is no match for the master deceiver. The entire world is following like sheep being led to slaughter. Therefore, I undertake this writing with a sense of urgency and hope that my voice will contribute to the prophetic message of the hour. Some of the revelations that I present in this writing will be the first time seeing them; I urge you to prayerfully consider what you are about to read. What I am about to share I believe to be a message directly from the heart of God.

What gives me the right to tackle these tough issues, and by what authority do I tackle these hard questions? "*... I am the voice of one crying in the wilderness ...*" (John 1:23). In this writing I upset the money tables, and challenge many of the doctrines, and forms of Christendom commonly accepted as being "the Church." I want my readers to understand that I do this with the full knowledge and understanding of the body of Christ and how it has evolved into the modern institution, "Church." I am compelled to publicly proclaim this new/old message, as the Apostle Paul wrote in Galatians, "*But I make known to you, brethren, that the gospel which was preached by me is not according to man. [12]For I neither received it from man nor was I taught it, BUT IT CAME THROUGH THE REVELATION OF JESUS CHRIST.*" (Galatians 1:11, 12, emphasis mine).

At one time I was a strong advocate for the "*Church.*" During my ministry my message was to proclaim, "*I am a church man; I love the church of Jesus Christ.*" One of my favorite scriptures to quote, Ephesians 5:27, "*... that he might present it to himself a glorious church, not having spot, or wrinkle, or any such thing; but that it should be holy and without blemish*" (KJV). My goal as a pastor has been to perfect the "church." I have pastored three congregations, been in the ministry for over forty-five years, and have been a minister in a major Pentecostal denomination. Most of my Christian life has been in church leadership; yet in spite of my service to Him, I realize that when a man earnestly seeks God and asks Him to show him His ways, that man must be ready for a new revelation!

As a student of the church, I have observed various practices and contradictions that have caused me to question, like why so many good Christians end up sidelined, and why miracles in the church have ceased. My search for truth has brought me to the conclusion that much of our established Christian doctrine is in error, and the church has become the purveyor of illusions. I have learned not to be afraid to investigate any and all sacred cows. In doing so, I have found it necessary to shoot a few of those sacred cows. In this book, I challenge established Christian doctrine and indulge my reader with prophetic revelation never before published in modern prophetic writing. I present a new perspective that I am confident is straight from the heart of YHWH God.

We are entering a new era in which the next move of God will not resemble anything we have ever seen before. A new wave is coming not only in the geo-political arena but more so in the spiritual dimension. People around the world are hungry for the next move of God but are not quite sure what it will look like. In this book, I have something new to say about the move of God that may make some people nervous; but for the earnest seeker, it will be a like a fresh glass of water. I am talking about YHWH God's ways—not man's ways. I do not attack the "church" simply to be critical; rather, this writing reveals a better way. This book is a must read for sincere seekers.

I am concerned that the development of the prophetic voice in the post-modern church has been influenced by a lying spirit. The prophetic destiny being purveyed is taking the world way off course and leading them into the judgments of God. Modern prophets have no vision from YHWH, and they propagate a misguided message wrapped around philosophies and doctrines that are self-indulgent and have neutered the church of its inherent power. Modern prophets and apostles' function more to keep "*the church on the reservation.*" These kinds of prophets are a dime a dozen and are surely leading the lambs to slaughter! Hence, the fabric of the "church" has been corrupted.

This writing I know will stretch my readers to the breaking point. I ask you to give this book a chance and reserve your judgment until you have read the whole document. In order to comprehend spiritual truth on the level it was intended, the seeker must be willing to have a change of perspective when confronted with new ideas. In order to come into the full revelation of YHWH's plans and purposes, the seeker is required to see through the eyes of God. As one of my teachers, Don Krider, stated: "*In order for us to understand the Word of God, we must have a relationship with the Author.*" My friend, this could be one of the most pivotal books of our present generation!

CHAPTER 1

THE SOVEREIGN SONS
OF YHWH

"Yours, O Lord [YHWH], is the greatness, the power and the glory, the
victory and the majesty;
For all that is in the heaven and in the earth is Yours;
Yours is the kingdom,
O Lord [YHWH], And You are exalted as Head above all."
(1 Chronicles 29:11)

ACCORDING TO YHWH's PLAN for planet earth, family groups are the heart of His plan. In Genesis ten, these family groups were strategically dispersed throughout the whole earth to populate and to prosper under His guidance. However, in opposition to YHWH's purpose to populate and restore the earth, tyrants arose out of these families to contradict His purposes. Nation/states arose out of these corrupted populations of sovereign families. From the foundations of the world Satan formulated a conspiracy to enslave humanity through governmental and religious institutions.

Unfortunately, humanity bought into his deception and has been brainwashed with the delusion that western civilization, democratic institutions and their religions are the true remedy for the world today. The cry for freedom around the world has been reduced to a cliché with people pitted against each other, struggling to find individual freedom and true destiny. In this expose, I will redirect seekers to the key to all history and the source of true sovereignty—into the liberty of the sons of God.

COME INTO MY FATHER'S TEEPEE

The title of this book, *Come into My Father's Teepee*, is YHWH's warm call inviting you to take a journey to return to Him and to become a part of His heavenly family. A wonderful illustration of the heavenly family is found in the traditional Blackfeet story of "Scarface," taken from the writings of George Bird Grinnell.[1] I have included a portion of the story as follows:

> …*Two swans came swimming up to shore and said to Scarface, "Why have you come here? What are you doing? It is very far to the place where your people live."*
>
> *"I have come here to die," replied Scarface. "Far away in my country is a beautiful girl. I want to marry her, but she belongs to the Sun; so I set out to find him and ask him for her. I have traveled many days. My food is gone. I cannot go back; I cannot cross this great water; so I must die."*
>
> *"No," said the swans; "it shall not be so. Across this water is the home of that Above Person. Get on our backs, and we will take you there."*
>
> *Scarface stood up. Now he felt strong and full of courage. He waded out into the water and lay down on the swans' backs, and they swam away. It was a fearful journey, for*

---

[1]   George Bird Grinnell, "Native American Legends, Blackfoot Legends–First Medicine Lodge," 1913, www.legendsofamerica.com/ na-medicinelodge.html, accessed 23 June, 2016.

that water was deep and black, and in it lived strange people and great animals which might reach up and seize a person and pull him down under the water; yet the swans carried Scarface safely to the other side. There was seen a broad, hard trail leading back from the water's edge.

"There," said the swans, "you are now close to the Sun's lodge. Follow that trail, and soon you will see it."

Scarface started to walk along the trail, and after he had gone a little way, he came to some beautiful things laying in the trail. There was a war shirt, a shield, a bow, and a quiver of arrows. He had never seen such fine weapons. He looked at them, but he did not touch them and at last walked around them and went on. A little further along, he met a young man, a very handsome person. His hair was long; his clothing was made of strange skins, and his moccasins were sewed with bright feathers.

The young man spoke to him and asked, "Did you see some weapons laying in the trail?"

"Yes," replied Scarface, "I saw them."

"Did you touch them?" said the young man.

"No," said Scarface; "I supposed someone had left them there, and I did not touch them."

"You did not meddle with the property of others," said the young man. "What is your name, and where are you going?" Scarface told him. Then said the young man, "My name is Early Riser (the morning star). The Sun is my father. Come, I will take you to our lodge. My father is not at home now, but he will return at night."

At length they came to the lodge. It was large and handsome, and on it were painted strange medicine animals. On a tripod behind the lodge were the Sun's weapons and his war clothing. Scarface was ashamed to go into the lodge, but Morning Star said, "Friend, do not be afraid; we are glad you have come."

3

When they went in a woman was sitting there, the Moon, the Sun's wife and the mother of Morning Star. She spoke to Scarface kindly and gave him food to eat, and when he had eaten, she asked, "Why have you come so far from your people?" So, Scarface told her about the beautiful girl that he wished to marry and said, "She belongs to the Sun. I have come to ask him for her."

When it was almost night and time for the Sun to come home, the Moon hid Scarface under a pile of robes. As soon as the Sun got to the doorway, he said, "A strange person is here."

"Yes, Father," said Morning Star, "a young man has come to see you. He is a good young man for he found some of my things in the trail and did not touch them."

Scarface came out from under the robes, and the Sun entered the lodge and sat down. He spoke to Scarface and said, "I am glad you have come to our lodge. Stay with us as long as you like. Sometimes my son is lonely. Be his friend..." [End snippet]

The story of Scarface continues and the Sun heals his scarred face, and finally, he is rewarded with his bride. The Blackfeet were called pagans because Christians believed they were sun worshippers; however, after examining traditional stories like Scarface, the evidence clearly reveals that they indeed worshipped the Creator God of whom the sun was symbolic. The swans called Him *"That Above Person."* The oral history of Native Americans is rich in prophetic pictures. If we prayerfully allow the Holy Spirit to teach us through them, they can be used to effectively evangelize indigenous people. Western civilization has sterilized Christianity and robbed humanity of much of its rich history in oral tradition.

The story of Scarface is a beautiful picture of the holy Trinity—the Father, the Son, and the Holy Spirit—dwelling together in the heavenly teepee. Sun told Scarface, *"Now soon you will go home. I wish to tell you something, and you must be wise and listen. I am the Chief, everything is mine; I made the earth, the mountains, the prairies, the rivers, and the forests; I made the people and all the animals. This is why I say I alone am Chief. I can never die."* Scarface's time spent in the Father's teepee was not an earthly encounter but a celestial encounter with the heavenly family. I can think of no greater revelation of the heavenly Family than that of Scarface. I have been a believer for a long time and I have never seen or heard a story of the heavenly Family as awesome as this one. The story goes on to describe his journey home. *"The Sun took Scarface to the edge of the sky, and they looked down and saw the world …The Sun showed him the short trail. It was the Wolf Road—the Milky Way. He followed it and soon reached the ground."*

The story of Scarface gives us a glimpse into the heavenly love fest of the Godhead, Father, Son and the Holy Spirit. Early Riser is an epiphany of Jesus who is our advocate with the Father, and He invites believers to enter the heavenly Father's teepee. Inside the teepee is warm and loving. Early Riser's mother, who is the Comforter, consoles Scarface and reaffirms him. In the Holy Spirit we find acceptance and affirmation. Inside the teepee there is acceptance and protection. Inside the teepee is everything needed to nurture and rear a family. In this writing, I am the swans inviting you to take the journey across the dark waters to find the trail that leads to our Father's teepee.

At some time in eternity past, the Godhead made a determination to create an intelligent being in their image who possesses a free will and can make a loving decision to become a part of the heavenly family. This company of sons and daughters joined together with the Godhead will complete the heavenly family for eternity. YHWH God's intention from the beginning of time is to have a family of sons and daughters who would share with them in the heavenly family, *"I will be a Father to you, and you shall be My sons and daughters, says YHWH God Almighty,"* 2 Corinthians 6:18.

The journey of Scarface to find the dwelling place of the Sun was driven by his desperation to marry his true love. Scarface is a type of you and I; he is a flawed individual, but his desperate love drives him to depart from the comforts of the village on a quest to find the trail that leads to the Sun's lodge, a place where he said, *"I do not know where I am going."* Scarface faced starvation and many dangers but persisted in his quest until he was exhausted, without provisions, with worn-out moccasins he surrendered to death. His story is not unlike the desperation of many believers in their pursuit to find their place with our heavenly Father. At last, when all hope was gone, Scarface was rescued by the swans.

We are living in an era when millions of believers are leaving the comforts of the mainline church and are seeking something real. Many do not know what that something is, yet they are desperate in their quest. Our journey in this writing takes us through the dangers and deceptions of the world, but, at last, we are given hope and comfort in the heavenly teepee of YHWH God. For those desperate to find the heavenly reality, we begin our journey by leaving our safety zones and beginning the quest to find true sovereignty.

WHAT IS SOVEREIGNTY?

"Again, the kingdom of heaven is like treasure hidden in a field, which a man found and hid; and for joy over it he goes and sells all that he has and buys that field."
(Matthew 13:44)

I was born and reared on the Blackfeet Indian Reservation and I was taught, like all other good First Nations people, that Indian reservations are sovereign countries. As a Native American and a student of history, I found it difficult to accept the illusion most Native Americans and their tribal governments have been led to believe. The basic assumption, that Indian reservations are sovereign nations, challenged me to investigate this assumption to see, if in fact, we really are sovereign. My journey, which has been through many years, has led me to conclude that not only have Native Americans been conned into believing they are sovereign, but even more stunning, I discovered that Christian religions and American society as a whole have been duped into believing they are sovereign.

We begin our journey by discussing *sovereignty*. It is necessary to make sovereignty our first priority because this is the fork in the trail where Christianity took the wrong turn early in its formation. God will bring us back to the same spot where the church took the wrong turn and abdicated her place of sovereignty. In order to re-claim the path that leads to Father's Teepee, it is necessary to go back and identify the right path. When one searches for the origin of individual or national sovereignty, it is necessary to transcend national and intellectual definitions, go beyond accepted explanations and find the true source of sovereignty. Like Scarface, we must be willing to cross the dark waters to find the path that leads to the truth. For believers to enter into the full experience of their salvation and God's kingdom, they must regain their inherent sovereignty. We begin our journey with a definition of sovereignty, this definition will put us on the path leading in the right direction.

> *Sovereignty is a precious gift granted to every son of man born into this world. It transcends the kingdoms of this world, and the governments of this world cannot grant sovereignty. Sovereignty is the state of being granted by YHWH God, where mankind has the freedom to exercise free will over individual matters. YHWH God's crown jewel of creation, mankind, has been given the free will to choose to be reinstated to the family of God and restored to their birthright and inheritance as children of YHWH.*

The English definition found in Wikipedia is as follows:

Sov•er•eign•ty/ˈsäv(ə)rəntē/noun: *sovereignty, supreme power, authority, and jurisdiction over self and individual matters*

Synonyms: *jurisdiction, rule, supremacy, dominion, power, ascendancy, suzerainty, hegemony, domination, authority, control, influence*

- a self-governing state, *a country's independent authority to govern itself*
- National sovereignty—*the authority of a state to govern itself or another state.*[2]

As a person searches for true sovereignty and is exposed to the chaotic condition of the world, he inevitably comes to the conclusion that humanity is a fallen kingdom! To aspire to find true sovereignty, every individual seeker must take responsibility for one's own life and cross the dark waters in order to find his place. The Apostle Paul warned believers to *"Stand fast in the liberty by which Christ has made us free, and do not be entangled again with the yoke of bondage"* (Galatians 5:1). In other words, the apostle was warning God's children not to settle for a form of sovereignty that is not genuine. The Enemy is a master counterfeiter, and he offers counterfeit liberty in many forms. We need to ask ourselves, where and when did we find sovereignty? And in what form did that sovereignty come?

If you have embraced a counterfeit, then your challenge is to change course, and in order to change course, you must have a change of heart and mind. The sincere seeker must alter his journey from the mind control and pressure to conform to regain control of his personal destiny. He must become

---

[2] "Sovereignty,"10 June 2016, *Wikipedia.com*, https://en.wikipedia.org/wiki/sovereignty, accessed 18 June 2016.

delivered from emotional and societal bondages. Doing so necessitates a change of mind. The battle is for your mind, and deception and confusion is the Enemy's playground. If he can convince you that you have sovereignty by handing you a counterfeit, then you are easy for him to control. You must be willing to change your mind and reform your way of thinking. This writing will present some new thoughts and concepts that will challenge you and will revolutionize you. I ask my readers to set aside their preconceived ideas and emotional dispositions and consider; maybe, just maybe...

An explorer came upon an Indian village on the Pacific coast and after inquiring learned that the name of the village was Oahu. When he queried about the name, he was told that he was in Hawaii. One of the elders spoke to him, *"A long time ago a man told us about Hawaii, so we began our journey west to find this paradise. He told us that Hawaii was the most beautiful place in the world; it was warm and had beautiful beaches and a blue ocean, palm trees and coconuts, and they were beautiful. When we arrived here, we said, 'This must be Hawaii because the beaches are beautiful, and the ocean is blue."*

When searching for the origin or the source of individual or national sovereignty, you must go beyond government and state to find the true source—*that land beyond the river.* A nation or state cannot grant you sovereignty they can only recognize it is the state of being endowed upon man by our Creator. A nation or a state can only recognize and honor the sovereignty that has already been granted to humanity by God. You cannot find liberty in riches. Education cannot give you sovereignty. Neither can religion—especially not religion— offer you liberty. Ultimately, every genuine search leads to the true source of sovereignty: a face-to-face relationship with the Creator of the universe—the One who is saying, *"I am who I am. I am the Chief; everything is mine. I made the earth, the mountains, the prairies, the rivers, and the forests; I made the people and all of the animals. This is why I say I alone am Chief. I can never die. I am Almighty God; there is no other!"* YHWH God is supreme, He is sovereign; He is the Most High God, the self-existent One, the Possessor of heaven and earth, and this my friend is the One who has the power to give you true sovereignty! "Only YHWH has the power to grant sovereignty by which we are given our birthright and the blessing; the birthright being Kingship anointing and the blessing being the Priesthood."

YHWH establishes two absolute realities; the first is that He is God, and there is no other, He and He alone is sovereign. *"I am the Lord* [YHWH] *your God, who brought you out of the land of Egypt, out of the house of bondage ..."* (Exodus 20:2). Read it again, and let it sink in: *"**I am YHWH your God ...**"* The second reality is that YHWH alone is responsible for transitioning the repentant from their condition of bondage into the state of being free men. There is no other source!

The One who creates is supreme. He who designs and makes the rules is sovereign. He has no source other than Himself. YHWH God is sovereign! He is supreme, and He answers to no one. He is the original Jurisdiction, the original Designer, the Architect, the supreme Authority, and He is the Originator of all. He is the Creator, the Possessor of heaven and earth. He owns everything, He makes the rules, and all things came out of Him and exist because of Him. *"You are worthy, O Lord, to receive glory and honor and power; for You created all things, and by Your will they exist and were created"* (Revelation 4:11).

The Sovereign God redeems believers, reinstates their birthright and endows them with sovereignty. As the Preamble of the United States Constitution states, *"We have been endowed with inalienable rights from the Creator."* The Sovereign God, through His grace and mercy delivers mankind from bondage and restores him to right standing, without fault as sons. The restoration of mankind's sovereignty is offered through the substitutionary sacrifice of YHWH's only begotten Son through His shed blood. This can only mean that the basis of individual sovereignty must be derived from an intimate face-to-face relationship with the **Creator God, through Jesus Christ**. True sovereignty then is the individual who has asked for and has been granted sovereignty from the Creator through Jesus. *"For whoever calls on the name of the Lord* [YHWH] *shall be saved"* (Romans 10:13).

YHWH's creation of mankind was framed for intimate relationship with no mediators, whether they are men, governments or religions. YHWH is looking for an exclusive relationship with you. Jesus said in Matthew 23:9, *"Do not call anyone on earth your father; for One is your Father, He who is in heaven."* In this verse Jesus is defining our exclusive relationship with our heavenly Father. Our walk is with God. Believers have been granted a face-to-face standing with the Creator of the universe. Sixteenth-century church reformers called it *coram Deo,* or *"all life is lived before the face of God."* We cannot allow any man or family, institution or government, science or religion come between us and our God. He supernaturally releases us from darkness and translates us into His family. *"… if anyone is in Christ, he is a new creation; old things have passed away; behold all things have become new"* (2 Corinthians 5:17).

Native American tribes in the beginning were created as sovereign First Nations, however, they were intentionally deceived by the government who usurped their inherent sovereignty, and in fact, they are under the exclusive jurisdiction of the United States government, and more specifically, the U.S. Senate, and the Bureau of Indian Affairs. Their legal status is as domestic dependent nations as declared by Chief Justice John J. Marshall. Indians have been duped to believe they are sovereign nations in order to appease them, but the intent behind the deception was to keep them on the reservations. The government did not want renegade Indians running around, causing problems by asserting their indigenous rights while America was busy establishing new jurisdictions over the land—jurisdictions appropriated from naïve Indians. "Let them think they are sovereign, but if they step out of line, the heavy hand of justice will *'keep them on the rez.'*

The *"keep-'em-on-the-rez"* deception is comparable to the paternal control of the modern-day "church." The intent behind the veil of deception is the same as the one perpetrated on the Indians: keep them in church but don't allow them to discover their true identity as the sons of YHWH. The church's intentional misleading that they are sovereign is described by Jesus in Matthew 23:13: "...*For you shut up the kingdom of heaven against men; for you neither go in yourselves, nor do you allow those who are entering to go in.*" In the same manner, today's modern church institution asserts freedom to its members, but in fact, the church has become an institution of bondage for God's children. The system is a veil of deception designed to pacify and blind believers away from true sovereignty. Pastors keep their congregations comfortable by telling them they are free people simply to keep them in the church as a cash cow. The intent is to make their members good citizens and churchgoers. Be good church members, pay your tithes, fill the pews, and be good citizens, but don't make waves. In other words, *"keep 'em-on-the-reservation."*

The new model of the heavenly family we are proposing is articulated in the original Greek by the word *oikos,* a primary doctrinal theme in the Bible that needs to be recovered. However, this doctrinal theme has been obscured and supplanted by the fraudulent founding of "the Church." The *oikos* concept of the heavenly family should alter the model of the western church into the model of the "heavenly family."

The institution of the church cannot produce the sons of YHWH. The "church" is a counterfeit of what YHWH intended for mankind; it was formulated as a diversion to sidetrack believers away from embracing the model of YHWH's family. The *oikos* model of the "heavenly family" will come more into focus in a later chapter.

When the true meaning of sovereignty is embraced, then YHWH declares His exclusive jurisdiction over His children. In the book of Numbers, chapter 6, YHWH instructed the priests to put His name upon them:

> *This is the way you shall bless the children of Israel. Say to them;* [24] *"The Lord [YHWH] bless you and keep you;* [25] *The Lord* [YHWH] *make His face shine upon you, and be gracious to you;* [26] *The Lord* [YHWH] *lift His countenance upon you, and give you peace [shalom]."* [27] *So they shall put My name on the children of Israel, and I will bless them"* (vv. 23-27).

The blessing formalized His exclusive jurisdiction over His children and endowed them with His shalom (supersized blessings) over their lives, this included their righteous standing as His sovereign sons. In the New Testament, the names of the Father, the Son and the Holy Spirit are placed upon the believer when they follow Him into the waters of baptism, which formalizes His relationship and establishes His exclusive jurisdiction over them (Matthew 28:19). We will elaborate on this in a latter chapter.

The inherent danger for the believer is to fall from their righteous standing in sovereignty. As believers, we are challenged to preserve our sovereignty and our righteous standing with our Father. We are tested by the First commandment, *"You shall have no other gods before Me"*(Exodus 20:3). A more accurate interpretation of the original Hebrew would be *"You shall put no other gods in front of My face or over My head.*" The apostle Paul exhorted believers to stand firm in the sovereignty they had been granted and warned them not to abandon their face-to-face relationship with YHWH by falling into situations where they put something else above God: "*Stand fast therefore in the liberty by which Christ has made us free, and do not be entangled again with a yoke of bondage*" (Galatians 5:1).

Modern Christians have been enculturated to a lifestyle of idolatry through comfortable living, self-indulgent religious systems, and paternalistic governments. Our natural reaction to this warning is, "Oh, I am a good person, I am not an idolater, I go to church, I am a good citizen, and I pay my taxes." The church is not much different than the children of Israel and I am afraid we will find ourselves under Jeroboam's sin and the same judgment. We don't realize that like ancient Israel, we have allowed our hearts to be filled with idol worship—from pop singers and athletes to our modern, comfortable lifestyles and religions. The prophet Ezekiel rebuked the elders of Israel in Ezekiel 14,

> *Now some of the elders of Israel came to me and sat before me. ²And the word of the Lord* [YHWH] *came to me, saying, ³"Son of man, these men have set up their idols in their hearts, and put before them that which causes them to stumble into iniquity. Should I let Myself be inquired of at all by them?⁴I ... will answer him who comes, according to the multitude of his idols, ⁵that I may seize the house of Israel by their heart, because they are all estranged from Me by their idols."*

Israel fell into idolatry and in the ways of Jeroboam and they refused to repent. Their obstinance resulted in God removing them from their homeland and driving them into all the countries of the earth. Please understand, the problem is not with God; rather, believers have unwittingly surrendered their sovereignty to false gods. God's answer to us is found in Isaiah 59:1, 2, which says, *"Behold, the Lord's [YHWH] hand is not shortened, that it cannot save; nor His ear heavy, that it cannot hear. ²But your iniquities have separated you from your God; and your sins have hidden His face from you, so that He will not hear."*

We, in the western world, are ignorant of the devices and schemes that Satan has devised to undermine our sovereignty—exactly like he did with Adam and Eve. One of the ways the Enemy steals our righteous standing is through our passive consent. We tacitly give our consent to others to act in our behalf, who then become our mediators, and we are held accountable for their actions. Christians passively and unwittingly relinquish their sovereignty to politicians, family members, religious authorities, government, habits and all forms of sins. Of course, consent is gained deceptively and illicitly by those in power who understand the principle that multiplied power comes by gaining the consent of dubious Christians, or should we say by usurping their sovereign authority. God's children fail to realize they must renounce all forms of unjust governmental and religious mediators who enslave them, conducting all sorts of unrighteous acts, such as war and abortion, on their behalf. Christians must realize they will stand accountable for the actions of their surrogates one day, and they must emphatically cling to their identity and sovereign authority.

I often say in my preaching, *"While we spend all of our lives trying to make ourselves comfortable living in this world, God has been working to make us uncomfortable in this world so that we can be comfortable in His kingdom."* If we are honest with ourselves, we come to the stark reality that even the Muslims show greater devotion to their god than we do to ours. Acts 1:8 says, *"But you shall receive power when the Holy Spirit has come upon you; and you shall be witnesses to Me ... to the end of the earth.*" The original Greek for *witness is martus,* this verse more accurately says, "*You shall be* <u>*martyrs*</u> *to Me to the ends of the earth.*" How many American Christians can truthfully declare they are willing to lay down their lives for the sake of the gospel? How many are willing to leave jobs, families, comforts and money for the sake of the gospel? How many are willing to repent and to come out from under unjust and unrighteous systems? Do we really possess the spirit of the martyrs? In order to regain true sovereignty, believers must regain their true identity as the sons of YHWH and separate from the spirit of Babylon.

When I was a young helicopter pilot being deployed to Vietnam, I was confronted with the thought that I may never return home alive. One of my best friends had already been killed in action, and my military occupation as a helicopter pilot had one of the highest casualty rates in the war. As I prepared to board the transport airplane, after saying goodbye to my loved ones, I died a death in my mind. I was willing to lay down my life! When you are a dead man walking, you transcend the fear of death. Do we really possess the spirit of the martyrs?

CHAPTER 2

THE EMERGENCE OF NATION/CITY STATES

"All nations whom You have made
Shall come and worship before you, O Lord [YHWH],
And shall glorify Your name.
[10]For You are great,
and do wondrous things;
You alone are God."
(Psalm 86:9, 10)

PEOPLE IN THE WESTERN world have been conditioned to give their loyalty and allegiance to the country of their citizenship as their source of freedom. We in the USA have been led to believe that good citizenship and service to our country are the highest ideals. As a young boy, I was led to believe that my highest goal in life was to become an "all- American boy." All of my life I was conditioned to believe that America was the highest form of freedom. I was a three-year letterman in football and a two-year letterman in basketball. I was my senior class president and student body president. I spent four years of my life in the United States Army and did a tour of duty in Vietnam as a combat helicopter pilot, fighting for what we believed was liberty. The whole culture of the United States of America is geared to condition children to believe that America is the ultimate form of liberty. Their strategy behind this conditioning is to keep the masses pacified, keep them entertained and preoccupied; in other words, *keep 'em fat and happy.*

The American church has been an accomplice in conditioning the psyche of its members and has walked dangerously close to idolizing America, preaching a message of nationalism and patriotism from its pulpits. How many times have you heard a message on Romans 13:1, *"Let every soul be subject to the governing authorities ..."*? Yet with all of its good intentions, the church has abdicated its sovereign standing and removed itself from her place of authority by spiritual fornication with government. Through incorporation and the 501(c)(3) tax-exempt status the "church" has elevated herself a new god over her head. We have entered an era where the fornication of church and state has ushered in "Mystery Babylon."

Every country on earth today is based on fraudulent claims of national sovereignty and this book challenges the legitimacy of the modern nation state's claims to sovereignty. Satan formulated a conspiracy from the beginning of time to enslave humanity through the emergence of satanically inspired, highly structured governmental and religious institutions. You could say that the nations of the earth are fictions of the law; they are creations of their own making. The emergence of nation/states on the face of the earth was basically a revolution against the will of YHWH, culminating in Mystery Babylon and in the near future, we will witness God's final judgment on the nations. Mankind's dispensation of rule is about to expire, more on that later.

It is a fundamental error to assume that God created every single nation on earth. Jesus defined this in Matthew

25:32 during His judgments on the nations. *"He will sit on the throne of His glory and all the nations will be gathered before Him, and He will separate them one from another ... He will set the sheep on His right hand and the goats on His left, He will say to those on His right hand, "Come you blessed of my Father, inherit the Kingdom prepared for you from the foundation of the world."* The identifying characteristics of God's nations is not for their good works but for the impartation of national sovereignty prepared for them from the foundation of the world. Psalm 86:9 *"All nations whom You have made shall come and worship before you, O YHWH."* The democratic nations of the world do not qualify for this condition because they are founded upon the consent of their people and do not represent God's sovereign rule on the earth. The marker of God's nations is that Jesus Christ the Son of YHWH is King and sole ruler! We must never lose our identity as citizens of the Kingdom of God.

Mankind has been allotted seven thousand years to rule on the earth. That time period was prophetically signified by the seven days of creation, as Peter declared that one day is as a thousand years. Mankind was allotted six thousand years with Jesus ruling for the final one-thousand-year Millenium reign however, mankind's rule was usurped by Satan in the Garden of Eden transferring their authority over the world to him resulting in his reign of terror. This six-thousand-year time period is shortly coming to an end, according to the calculations of many end-time eschatologists, with four thousand years before Christ and two thousand years after the cross coming to a close. The appearance of the Sign of the Son of Man in the heavens, spoken by Jesus, will mark the end of the Times of the Gentiles. More about this in the last chapter, **"Time Is Short"**. King Jesus is coming with all power and authority. Oh, foolish kings and sovereigns, have you not read Psalm 2, the end of your time is rapidly approaching. This includes the United States. It amazes me to see Christians and their so-called prophets proclaiming the Great Awakening and re-emergence of Constitutional rule over the USA when the commission by Jesus to His followers is the proclaim the Kingdom of God.

We are witnessing the disintegration of many so-called sovereign nations around the world; and in the near future, we will witness the shattering of all nations (Revelation 16:19, Daniel 2:34, Psalm 2:9). Nearly every government in the world today is operating in breach of legitimacy, abusing the power granted to it by the people, including the so-called democratic governments of the world. What is going on? How could powerful nation states come to nothing? Our assertion in this writing is the nations of the earth are in rebellion against the Creator and have been operating on the pretense of legitimacy. The people of the world are being held in deception by the nations and are being incited to war against YHWH. Yet in spite of the chaos, we are living in the time when YHWH's order will be established. Oh, foolish kings and sovereigns, have you not read Psalm 2?

Why do the nations rage and the people plot a vain thing? ²The kings of the earth set themselves, and the rulers take counsel together, Against the Lord [YHWH] and against His Anointed, saying, ³"Let us break Their bonds in pieces and cast away Their cords from us."
⁴He who sits in the heavens shall laugh; the Lord [YHWH] shall hold them in derision.
⁵Then He shall speak to them in His wrath, and distress them in His deep displeasure:
⁶"Yet I have set My King on My holy hill of Zion."
⁷"I will declare the decree: the Lord [YHWH] has said to Me, ' You are My Son, Today I have begotten You.
⁸Ask of me, and I will give You the nations for your inheritance, And the ends of the earth for Your possession.
⁹You shall break them with a rod of iron; You shall dash them to pieces like a potter's vessel.' "
(Psalm 2:1-9)

Where do the nations find the right to call themselves *sovereign?* The conventional assumption is they obtain their legitimacy from their sovereign citizens. If you look at the basis of the US Constitution, which was modeled after the Mayflower Compact, you find that the covenants were with the citizens and not under God; although, they used the name of God; i.e. "*We the people … in order to form a more perfect union.*" If so, where do the people find the right to call themselves sovereign, if, in fact, they are still in bondage? However, our assertion is that they are in rebellion against the Creator, and their claims based on ILLEGITIMATE sovereignty and they are creations of their own making.

> During the 1600s the royal families of England were bringing out the principle known as the DIVINE RIGHTS OF KINGS—in other words it was declared right for them to reign and what they said or did was God-given. The principle of The God-given Right to Govern Vested in the Sovereign Authority of the Whole People was a radical idea and one that met much opposition from the reigning kings of that time.[3]

The founders of nations have wrestled with the logic of who has the legitimate right to govern. Unfortunately, unredeemed mankind does not have the sovereign right to establish government apart from God. This question has resulted in instability and warfare throughout history. Also, with the assumed God-given right of the whole people to govern, comes the right for them to tear it down if they were not satisfied.

You could say that the nations of the earth are fictions of the law, or in other words, they are not established on

---

3 Frank Dietz, "Twenty-Eight Principles that Helped Build America," 15 April 2016, https://twitter.com/frankdietz/status/720941769689423872, accessed 17 June 2016.

universal legitimacy, but on unfounded foundational premises. The emergence of nation/states on the face of the earth was basically a revolution against the will and purposes of YHWH. Nation/states arose out of the populations of the original Genesis chapter ten sovereign families of the earth, whom YHWH had commissioned to populate and replenish the earth. According to YHWH's plan for planet earth family groups or tribes were sent to populate the earth and flourish under His jurisdiction and guidance. Out of these families, tyrants emerged to contradict His purposes. From the beginning of time Satan formulated a conspiracy to enslave humanity through the emergence of satanically inspired highly structured government and religious institutions.

THE ORIGIN OF NATION/STATES

Behold, the nations are as a drop in a bucket,
And are counted as the small dust on the scales …
[17]All nations before Him are as nothing, (fictions)
And they are counted by Him less than nothing and worthless.
[18]To whom then will you liken God?
(Isaiah 40:15-18)

In Genesis chapters ten and eleven, two trees of governmental systems emerged in the earth, into prototypes of future governmental systems: one tree emerged under the rule of YHWH God into the sovereign First Nations, and the second tree emerged under the rule of man or more specifically Satan. We will call this new counter movement "The Reign of Force," or as George Washington defined government, "*Government is not reason, it is not eloquence; it is force! Like fire, it is a dangerous servant and a fearful master.*"[4] According to

---

[4]   "Police Dynamics: Power for Effective Law Enforcement," 25 March, 2011, (https://policedynamics.wordpress. com/2011/o3/o5/gov), accessed 17 June 2016.

YHWH's plan, family groups strategically populated the earth in order to reestablish His order. These First Nations were identified by four characteristics in Genesis 10 that defined them as nations: *"From these the coastland peoples of the Gentiles were separated* **[1] into their lands, [2] everyone according to his language, [3] according to their families, and [4] into their nations"** (Genesis 10:5, 20, 31, 32, NKJV).

1. ***"People separated into their lands"*:** Each family group was gifted by Creator with an inheritance—an area of land where they could live and flourish under His blessing and guidance. The Bible doesn't clearly say how each group arrived in his homeland, but we can presume they were transported by the Holy Spirit in the way of His choosing, whether it was by boat, by foot, by air, or by the hand of God:

   "... by these the isles of the Gentiles were divided in their lands" (v. 5, KJV).

   "... and from these the nations were divided on the earth after the flood" (v. 32).

Most Native American emergence stories begin during or after the "Great Flood," where they emerge in their indigenous homelands. The oral tradition and collective memory of individual tribal groups originate in their indigenous homelands, contrary to the "land bridge" theory offered by archeology. Don't confuse their land inheritance with land ownership because the concept of ownership was not a part of God's plan, and neither did indigenous tribes adhere to the concept of land ownership. *"Get out of your country, from your family and from your father's house, to a land that I will show you. ²I will make you a great nation ..."* (Genesis 12:1-2). Tribal groups or families were given indigenous homelands not to own or possess; YHWH is the exclusive owner of His creation, but sovereign families were keepers of YHWH's blessings. Land ownership originated with the rise of feudal kingdoms as we will address later.

2. **"According to his language":** Each ethnic group was gifted with a unique cultural language that contained the DNA of the Creator, so that each group could communicate with Him and worship Him in their culturally unique way. While attending a conference of the World's Indigenous People in Hilo, Hawaii, my whole world was rocked by the beauty I heard in the language and songs of the Hawaiians. I was amazed and touched by the beauty of the words with which they had been gifted to glorify God. My imagination drifted to the thought that if their language was a gift to glorify God, then why not the language of my people, the Blackfeet? This thought inspired me to learn the language of my people, and as I did, I was flooded with emotions, like I was coming home! It was like my language was comfortable; it fit. Even though I may not be fluent in my language, I rejoice in the spirit I feel when using my language. Through their languages, the tribes were able to maintain their cultural identity through oral tradition. It was through the distinctive expression of their tribal language that made them unique to the Creator who communicated with each group through their language.

3. **"According to their families":** In a later chapter, we will go in-depth in the study of God's plan for the family, which is near and dear to His heart. Families— social structures, cultures, and tribes—were identified by their national colors, clothing, symbols, teepees, languages and cultural traits. Each group developed a social structure (culture), which centered on the worship of the Creator. Each culture was distinct and carried

the DNA of YHWH so that each group glorified the Creator in a unique way that only that particular cultural group could. Through community worship, the divine will and mind of YHWH was imparted to the people, thus establishing the rule of God and His economy. Even to this day the "HAYAH" is sung by Native Americans in their celebrations. This is evidence of their connection with the post Flood First Nations of the Creator who revealed Himself to them as the HAYAH. In addition, many Paleo Hebrew inscriptions have been found at First Nations sites around the world.

I believe that the reason Satan hates Native Americans and has tried so hard to exterminate tribal culture is because First Nations cultures is one of the last remaining traditions of YHWH's original design. Satan's hatred of indigenous cultures has provoked civilization and religion to destroy the traditional ethnos of the Genesis. Even the modern Christian church has acted as accomplices in the destruction of indigenous cultures. The early missionary mindset was that natives were savages, calling them *pagan*, and demanding indigenous people to reject their cultures and to melt into the mixing pot of Western civilization. I always say, *"Jesus did not come to destroy culture; He came to destroy the works of the Devil."*

The Blackfeet were distinctive in their designs and graphics painted on their teepees. The artwork on Blackfeet lodges tells a story older than the United States, going back to the very beginning of Creation. Only the Bible can compare to the ancient history that is preserved in the painting on Blackfeet teepees. The Blackfeet were famous for their colorful painted lodges. When a rider approached an encampment, he identified the band by the designs painted on the lodges, much like the distinct skylines of modern cities. Lodges were not simply painted at random but were depictions of visions and encounters the lodgers had experienced. The beautiful artwork lodge designs of the Blackfeet are sacred and cannot be sold or given to people who are not authorized to use them; they represent supernatural encounters of the lodgers, and the design was handed down through the generations. The Blackfeet teepees were divided into three distinct sections: the top, the middle and the bottom. These three sections were symbolic of the separation of the Star People from the Earth People that occurred during the great flood.

The top dark section of the teepee represents the life before the flood. Blackfeet believe that, in the beginning, the Earth people and the Star people, or Holy people, dwelled upon the earth and coexisted in a peaceful and serene existence. The Earth people became corrupted and became very wicked and sinful, which greatly grieved the Star people and so offended them that they left the earth and returned to the heavens and became the stars we see in the night sky. The white circles or stars around the top dark section of the teepee symbolize the Star People. Blackfeet tribal migrations were guided by the Star People. In Christianity, the star people could be referred to as *angels* or *saints*.

The light-colored middle section represented the water of the great flood that came upon the earth and destroyed the wicked Earth people; it can also represent the sky or the vast cosmos that separates the Star people from the Earth people. The teepees have paintings of otters, beavers, fish or other animals that represent the power symbols of the lodgers or were the animals that helped Napi (Blackfeet for "Old Man") recreate the Earth after the flood. Most Blackfeet origin stories begin with Napi sending the animals deep into the waters to bring up mud he used to create the ground. These ancient stories tell about the creation of Chief Mountain and the Sweet Grass Hills, the Milk River, and many other landmarks that can be seen today. Although the exact details differ from the Christian creation story, the basic concepts parallel the biblical creation story. The bottom dark section of the lodges represents the earth or the ground that mankind dwells upon. This section usually has peaks which are the mountains or hills and the many white circles represent the humans that dwell on the earth today. It is the lower dark section that humanity experiences.

"Blackfeet Teepee"

4. **"*Into their nations*":** Each family group was endowed with a divine impartation of national sovereignty and was given exclusive jurisdiction over their inheritance in order to flourish in their land as indigenous people. The word *nations* in this context, in the original Hebrew, implies "national sovereignty or national authority." Therefore, using the term "First Nations" accurately describes these groups, "*...For there is no authority except from God, and the authorities that exist are appointed by God,*" (Romans 13:1). Power or governmental jurisdiction was imparted to sovereign people groups who walked with YHWH. The tribal cultures revolved around the worship and obedience to the Creator or Great Spirit who imparted governmental guidance to them. "*All nations whom You have made shall come and worship before you, O Lord* [YHWH]" (Psalm 67:6).

These are the true sovereign First Nations. For example, Native American councils gathered around fires and council tents to seek the divine will and wisdom of the Great Spirit. The Blackfeet called Him *Itsibatibiopa* or "*the one who provides everything we have need of.*" This concept of theocratic government is illustrated within indigenous cultures, including the Blackfeet people who followed a patriarchal system that honored the *Ninna* or "Father." In the tipi, the father *(Ninna)* was honored; it was his sole domain. Everything in the tipi was geared around the *Ninna.* Tribal elders or grandfathers were honored as *Ninna,* and the clan chief or leader of the group was honored as *Ninna*; they, in turn, honored and prayed to the Heavenly Father or *Ninna who provided divine guidance.*

Another example of a tribal social structure that worshipped the Creator was known as the "Prophet Movement." The Plateau tribes of the Northwest followed a system of theocratic government that revolved around holy men, or prophets, who would seek God for divine guidance. When the prophet received a revelation or message from the Great Spirit, he would call for a gathering of the people. The people would come and form a circle. From the center, the prophet would deliver the message. The people would then begin to sing and dance in place until the Spirit came and confirmed the message. One of the earliest recorded revelations came from the Spokane Prophet Silimxnotylmilakobok:

> *I will send messengers to earth by the souls of the people that reach me, but whose time to die has not yet come. They will carry messages to you from time to time; and when their souls return to their bodies, they will revive, and tell you their experiences. Coyote and Myself will not be seen again until the Earth-Woman is very old. Then we will return to earth, for it will require a new change by that time.*

Coyote will precede me by some little time and when you see him, you will know the time is at hand. When I return, all spirits of the dead will accompany me. All the people will live together. Then will the Earth-Woman revert to her natural shape, and live as a mother among her children, then will things be made right, and there will be much happiness.[5]

This practice developed later on into the "Ghost Dance" and what is known as the "Jump Dance." Each tribal group flourished as they followed the governing authority of YHWH God in the land of their inheritance.

NIMROD, THE RULE OF FORCE

The counterfeit power structure that emerged in the earth came through *force,* under the hand of a powerful man named Nimrod. The name *Nimrod* (Hebrew—*gibbower*) is defined as "tyrant, warrior, mighty hunter,"or as a king "dictator"; i.e.,"rule by force." Scripture states that Nimrod "*...began to be a mighty one on the earth*" (Genesis 10:8). The word *mighty* is used twice in reference to Nimrod and in the original language literally means "a tyrant or dictator."This interpretation may indicate that Nimrod was not only the first empire-building ruler or king, but that he possessed supernatural satanic powers. According to the book of Jasher he received supernatural power from his undergarments that his father Cush stole from Noah. His powers certainly were not originally recognized by YHWH because he practiced a totally idolatrous religious system with himself as the sovereign god/king. The power source of this movement was counterfeit and was birthed out of force or tyranny and

---

[5]   Leslie Spier, *The Prophet Dance of the Northwest and Its Derivatives: The Source of the Ghost Dance* (Menasha, Wis.: George Banta Publishing Co., 1935), p. 11.

bears all of the traits of its master, the Devil. The root of the counterfeit is the master usurper of authority, Satan himself. *"Cush begat Nimrod: he began to be a mighty one on the earth… [10]the beginning of his kingdom was Babel, Erech, Accad, and Calneh, in the land of Shinar. From that land he went to Assyria and built Nineveh, Rehoboth Ir, Calah,…[12](that is the principal city)"* (Genesis 10:8-12).

This second tree of governmental structure emerged out of illegitimate or counterfeit authority that was appropriated by force; or to use superior physical or mental power to make somebody do something, i.e., the armed forces, the police force, the force of nature, etc., or by empire building and conquest of indigenous people groups. Nimrod usurped sovereign authority from the "First Nations," as they surrendered sovereignty for safety and security. All sources of so-called sovereign authority of modern nations and their counterfeit jurisdiction have been usurped from indigenous people groups of the earth.

In Genesis 10:10, *"… the beginning of his kingdom,"* the Hebrew word for *beginning* (*re'shiyth*) indicates "the first in place or time or order of origin," which means that Nimrod was the first god/king. His kingdom was the template of authoritarian rule by "monarchy," or God/kings, that has been practiced down through the ages, i.e. "the divine right of kings." Verse 11 says, *"From that land he went …"* The words *"he went"* are not a passive term referring to "a casual stroll," but in all actuality means he took his conquest from there and went to conquer other cities and tribes in order to expand his empire. Notice the reference to *"His kingdom or "his empire."* The use of the word "his" is possessive and implies ownership or the beginning of land ownership by kings, as opposed to YHWH's. The rule of monarchs throughout the ages has been identified by the same characteristics employed by Nimrod.

These two systems of government came into a clash with the arrival of Europeans in the Americas. In Noah's "Division of Nations" he said, *"May God enlarge Japheth, and may he dwell in the tents of Shem.*" The prophecy was fulfilled as Europeans, the descendents of Japheth, began to occupy the land of the First Nations, the descendant of Shem. Had they honored the generosity of the First Nations and co-existed in their teepees the propagation of the gospel would have been accomplished; instead, Japheth decided to stay on and claim it for himself. The rule of force compelled them to drive the Native people out of their inheritance and to occupy their land, resulting in First Nations living as second-class citizens in their own lands.

TRAITS OF NATIONS/CITY STATES

- Governments of man are in rebellion against the rule of YHWH God

- Force or tyranny originated from Satan to establish his counterfeit order

- All so-called sovereign authority claimed by modern nations is illegitimate

- Gentile rule originated from man; man is the head

- All nations have emerged out of force, power or deception

- Rule of law, or rule by force, subjugates the citizens

- The concept of land ownership originated with monarchies

"Tyrants wish to usurp God's authority. Thus, their lusts and desires for rule over others run antithetical to the economy and administration of the Almighty."

"The halls of tyranny are the abode of demons and haters of God. But God will not be mocked. Tyrants and those who enable them will lose their souls, but even before that, time isn't on their side. Tyrants will be held accountable both in time and eternity."

*Every high thing must come down. Every stronghold shall
be broken He wears the Victor's crown*

He shall overcome He shall overcome

*Be of strong heart and good cheer. You are not on the losing
side.* [6]

THE CITY STATE/BABYLON

PHASE TWO OF COUNTERFEIT governmental systems was the
beginning of democracy in Babel, the prototype form of the city/
state, which eventually evolved into nation states and finally climaxes in
a one-world government. Notice the phrase in Revelation 16:19,
"... and the cities of the nation's fell." The traits of Babel's
city/states is carried on from Babel to Revelation, representing
sovereign entities outside of God's jurisdiction.

In Genisis chapter 11, the people found a plain in the
land of Shinar, and there they gathered as an autonomous
group and incorporated a municipality for the purpose of
opposing the will of God, (Genesis 11:2). As a cohesive unit, they
believed they could establish their own jurisdiction apart from the
rule of YHWH. Thus, the beginning of the city/state was an act
of rebellion against the divine order of Creator. " ... *Come,
let us build ourselves a city, and a tower whose top is in the heavens:
let us make a name for ourselves, lest we be scattered abroad ..."*
(Genesis 11:4). The phrase *"let us build ourselves"* specifies it
was their own plan apart from the will of God, a deliberate
revolt against YHWH's order, to create their own institution. The
phrase, *"lest we be scattered ..."* indicates their resistance to the
plan of YHWH. Where Nimrod had forged a kingdom by force,

---

[6] Herschel Smith, "The Captain's Journal: Bureau of Land Management Versus
Cliven Bundy," 13 April 2014, *The Captain's Journal,* http:// www.captainsjournal.
com/2014/04/13/bureau-of-land-management-versus-cliven-bundy-post-
mortem/, accessed 17 June 2016.

the city/state was a collaborative effort; they stopped in a place of their own choosing, and the multi- ethnic people group joined forces and came together as one, i.e., *We the People of the United States, in Order to form a more perfect Union ...*"

The "Out-of-Many-One" concept is the antithesis of YHWH's order and has been institutionalized as the basis of modern democracy. *"The power of the One, according to God's plan, is, "out of One God many nations"; according to man's plan, "out of many people one nation."*[7] The same traits of democratic governments have been carried on through the ages. However, in a democracy God's theocratic order is overruled and the rule of man is instituted. This is where the mind of the spirit is needed to discern the difference between the divine order of the kingdom of God and the pressure of society to impose rule by law.

Genesis chapter eleven begins, *"Now the whole earth had one language and one speech"* (v. 1). Down through the ages, theologians have taught that only one language existed in the earth before the founding of Babel; however, the context of chapters ten and eleven clearly shows that each *First Nations* had his own specific language, culture, land and nation. In addition, all people groups shared an ancient common language, the language of creation, that had been retained through the flood. This was the pre flood Paleo Hebrew, the language of creation. This common language aided differing peoples coming together as "one" in order to establish and build Babylon. *"...Indeed, the people are one and they all have one language, and this is what they begin to do; now nothing that they propose to do will be withheld from them,"* (Genesis 11:6). The Aleph Beht is powerful and formed the Paleo language which was the foundation of the Logos of creation. From this original Paleo language YHWH was able to pass on the original creation story of Genesis. In Genesis 11:7 God says, *"Come, let Us go down and there confuse their language*

..." The word *language* is singular, indicating it was *one* language. God's judgment was simple: remove the DNA of the original language. The confusion of languages was globally catastrophic and confused the origin stories of the indigenous people groups around the world.

Historical records indicate Babylon was a city in the ancient Sumerian civilization, which was one of the largest and most sophisticated countries of that time. Sumer is known as "the cradle of civilization" or "the birthplace of Western Civilization." It was there that the descendants of Shem occupied and dominated. The beginning of democracy arose out of Babel and the ancient civilization of Sumer— "*Come let us build ourselves a city.*" A *city* is "a municipality, the origin of civilization, defined as life in the city." "*Come let us ...*" implies that the people chose to establish their own entity or an identity apart from God. Let's follow the steps the people of Babel would have logically taken to establish their own municipality.

To establish order, the first step was to enter into a covenant in the form of *incorporation*— "a formalized covenant of organization or control; *Incorporated*—adj. formed or united into a whole, organized and maintained as a legal corporation." All governments are corporations, and a city is "a covenant or incorporated municipality or jurisdiction formed by a group of citizens to be governed by their consent. *Incorporation*— The act of uniting several persons into one fiction called a corporation, in order that they may be no longer responsible for their actions."[8]

The first article of the Articles of Incorporation is to declare the name of the new entity; by changing the name, a new identity is established, meaning you change your identity. "*Come ... let us make a name for ourselves ...*" (Genesis 11:4). By changing their name, they rejected the

---

[8]   Ambrose Bierce, 1885.

identity YHWH had given and the corporation to became their new identity, making His law of none effect in their lives. They changed their identity as sons of God to become Babylonians. To regain true sovereignty, one must repent of the Babylonian system to regain their true identity as the sons of YHWH.

The next entry in the articles of incorporation is the new address; they changed the address God had chosen to the new place of their municipality. Their old address placed them under God's jurisdiction; the change of address removed them from His jurisdiction to that of the city. They became *citizens*— "a member of a state who owes their allegiance to its government." *Citizenship* is "the state of being vested with the rights and duties of a citizen." By becoming citizens, they relinquished their rights as First Nations people. They chose to reject the life given to them by YHWH in exchange for a civil life in the community. Western civilization has been based upon this method of ordering citizens to comply with the advanced state of human society. They became good citizens, or should we say, *civilized*.

The next step in incorporating is to declare its purpose. The purpose of Babylon was to found a city and a religion *whose* purpose was to rebel against the Almighty: "...*let us build ourselves a city, and a tower whose top is in the heavens; let us make a name for ourselves, lest we be scattered abroad over the face of the whole earth*" (Genesis 11:4). In the original language, the tower whose top is in the heavens implies "a shaking of the head," which is a defiant act toward God. In addition, the name Bab-El means, the gateway of the Gods. By establishing their own religion and system of sacrifice, they were resisting the worship of the Creator to worship an entity of their own choosing. It is logical to assume that blood sacrifice was made to dedicate the tower. Also, their purpose for the religion/city was to resist God's command to send them into the earth to spread His dominion. Babylonian worship is essentially the worship of man, or, when more clearly defined, the worship of self; man is his own god independent of YHWH.

Finally, *incorporation* declares the ownership structure of the entity; they rejected the ownership of God and asserted their ownership by the state; they removed themselves from YHWH's ownership to a status of ownership by the city. Their declaration of ownership reveals to us that the concept of property, and land ownership by men and state had already been in practice for some time.

> *YOUR GOVERNMENT uses force to extract resources from YOU, and if you don't submit to, and obey its laws and programs, it will fine you, jail you and kill you, which, BECAUSE your government is an OCCUPYING FORCE AT HOME, it has the perfect right-of-a-conquering-government-nation to do it—THE SPOILS OF WAR IS TO OWN CITIZENS.*[9]

"*So, the Lord* [YHWH] *scattered them abroad from there over the face of all the earth, and they ceased building the city.* [9]*Therefore its name is called Babel, because there the Lord* [YHWH] *confused the language of all the earth; and from there the Lord* [YHWH] *scattered them abroad over the face of all the earth*" (Genesis 11:8, 9). The judgment on Babel was globally catastrophic because of the confusion of languages, and in Revelation 18:21, the Bible describes God's judgment upon Mystery Babylon and the devastation where no trace will be left of her: "*…Thus with violence the great city of Babylon shall be thrown down, and shall not be found anymore.*"

---

[9]   T. T. Braun, 32.

SPIRITUAL BABYLON

BABYLON is the spiritual fabric of iniquity; the mystical great city of the great king of darkness; built in imitation of Zion, painted just like Zion, that it might be taken for Zion, and be worshipped there, instead of the true, eternal, ever living God, and King of Zion.[10]

The challenge for today's Christians is to discern between spiritual Babylonian and Mount Zion, the dwelling place of the Great King YHWH.*"But you have come to Mount Zion and to the city of the living God, the heavenly Jerusalem..."* (Hebrews 12:22). The problem we are encountering is a generation of Christians who have become desensitized to the things of the Holy Spirit. While we have been trying to get God to come into our churches, He has been trying to get us to come into His house. Religion is the magic potion given to drink in order to scratch religious cravings and to get rid of their guilt complexes. The church has become Satan's weapon of choice to neuter Christians and to desensitize them of their inherent power. Believers must be set free from the mind control of religion and the pressure to conform.

We must keep in mind that we are speaking of precedents: monarchies arising out of Nimrod and city/states arising out of Babylon. The only reason God emphasized the city of Babel was because of the precedent set for the coming ages. From its inception, Babel represented the antithesis of the kingdom of God: *"the mystical great city of the great king of darkness."*[11] Whereas, Jesus came to build the kingdom of God, Satan established Babylon as an imitation or *an illusion* of God's order. Satan's established order of Babylon is the antithesis of God's order so he can build his counter-kingdom on the earth.

---

[10] Isaac Penington, *Writings from the Kingdom of God*, accessed 18 June 2016.

[11] Penington.

Out of Babel emerged not only false governmental authority structures but also false religious forms and idolatrous schemes of worship. The name *Babylon* in the ancient Sumerian culture meant "the gateway of the gods" or *Bab-El*.[12] Babel was the birthplace of iniquity, *"For the mystery of iniquity is already at work ..."* (2 Thessalonians 2:7) KJV. The master deceiver played his trump card by capitalizing on the *"mystery of iniquity,"* the adulterous spirit within the darkened hearts of mankind, which provokes worshipers to idolatry. Under the guise of religion, the mystical spirit of Babylon has committed spiritual fornication with the kings of the earth, and the inhabitants of the earth have been made drunk with the wine of her fornication, Revelation 17:2. Under the guise of being good, Babylon has deceived the inhabitants of the earth into worshipping Satan through false religions, false governmental systems, and false gods. *"All who dwell on the earth shall worship him* [the Dragon], *whose names have not been written in the Book of Life of the Lamb slain from the foundation of the world"* (Revelation 13:8). Babylon has deceived the people, and in today's world, provoke citizens to war against the rule of YHWH. Citizens worship the almighty government and believe that governments—not God—provide for all of the huddled masses.

The unique aspect of Babel and the rallying point for the people was the merger of state and religion through the building of the tower of Babel, *"Come, let us build ... a tower whose top is in the heavens"* Genesis 11:4. Please keep in mind that the logic behind establishing state religion is for more efficient control of the citizenry. The beginning of organized religion in Babel was designed to divert worship away from the Creator and to control the populace. By uniting church and state, religion can be used to control its members by making

---

[12] "Babylon the Harlot," www.discoverrevelation.com/9.html, accessed 18 June 2016.

them into good citizens and bringing them under the power of the state, i.e., *"Let every soul be subject to the governing authorities"* Romans 13:1. Religion is derived from the Latin word *legion*, in the military sense, *"to come into order or to gather into ranks,"*[13] or more specifically, "re-legion." Remember the order and the ranks of the Roman legions?

The tower of Babel was an altar to their new deity, Satan. The *tower* or "ziggurat, pyramid" was constructed of manmade bricks building an altar to the efforts of man. According to God's order of worship, altars were to be constructed of natural stones never touched by the chisel or the hand of man. Altars were symbolically a place of sacrifice, surrender and covenanting with God. In the Old Testament, altars were a type of the cross where surrender and sacrifice to Jesus was the order of worship. The tower of Babel was a perversion of God's divine order where blood sacrifices were made to foreign gods.

Many believers today are waiting for the Great Tribulation to usher in Mystery Babylon at some future date. This kind of spiritual desensitizing has blinded Christian not to discern they are currently living under a spirit of Babylon. I am looking forward to the day when we hear the call from anointed preachers: *"…Come out of her, my people, lest you share in her sins, and lest you receive of her plagues"* (Revelation 18:4).

---

[13] "Legion," *Dictionary.com*, www.dictionary.com/browse/legion, accessed 18 June 2016.

CHAPTER 3

THE BEGINNING OF THE
FAMILY OF GOD

Sing to God, sing praises to His name;
Extol Him who rides on the clouds,
By His name YAH,
And rejoice before Him.
5A father of the fatherless
A defender of widows,
Is God in His holy habitation,
6God sets the solitary in families;
He brings out those who are bound into prosperity ...
(Psalm 68:4-6)

GENESIS CHAPTER TWELVE BEGINS with YHWH's
command to Abram to get out of his country and from his people
to a land "*...I will show you*" (Genesis 12:1). Abram originally
came from Mesopotamia, apparently fleeing the collapse of the
Sumerian Empire and the subsequent chaos that history records
as a result of a climatic disaster. We can logically connect the
disaster in Sumer to the judgment that had befallen the tower
of Babel. Apparently, the trauma that accompanied the
collapse of the tower of Babel, the confusion of languages,
and the subsequent dispersion of the people was globally
traumatic. "*So, the Lord scattered them abroad from there over the*

face of all the earth ... ⁹there the Lord confused the language of all the earth ...Genesis 11:8, 9.

Abraham's father, Terah, lived in Ur of the Chaldees, a famous Chaldean city in the land of Sumer on the Euphrates River, serving as one of Nimrod's advisors. Terah was a serial idolater and it was from there Abraham departed to establish a new nation, one that would reestablish God's dominion in the earth. We can deduce from this portion of scripture that many First Nations had succumbed to the influence of the "Rule of Force" and God called Abram to be His spearhead to father a new nation. Through this new nation all the families of the earth would be blessed (Genesis 12:1-3). According to Douglas Elwell in his book, **Planet X, The Sign of the Son of Man and the End of the Age:** *"Abraham, when he fled Ur, took with him the only truly accurate version of the ancient Creation tradition, the version that would later be used by Moses and the prophets for all the Creation material to be found in the Old Testament."*[14]

God's command to Abram, *"I will make you a great nation; I will bless you and make your name great; and you shall be a blessing ...³And in you all the families of the earth shall be blessed"* (Genesis 12:2, 3), was an impartation of divine sovereign governmental authority. This portion of scripture is taught as the Abrahamic Blessing is actually the legal founding of a new nation: *"I will make you a great nation..."* (v. 2). This is a vital concept to grasp in understanding the development of nations and nation/states. YHWH's impartation of national sovereignty to Abram came from YHWH whereas the nations of the earth base their sovereignty on a fiction of law. There was an impartation of national sovereignty given to Abram and he was authorized to establish a new

---

[14]   Douglas Elwell, *Planet X, The Sign of the Son of Man and the End of the Age* (Crane, MO: Defender Publishing, 2010).

dispensation of sovereign rule on planet earth. All of the four elements establishing the First Nations in Genesis 10 and 11 are included in this blessing: 1) Land, 2) Culture (family), 3) National sovereignty, and 4) Language.

The only item not mentioned in the blessing is language; however, we can deduce from scripture that Abram, a direct descendant of Shem, carried the DNA of the original Paleo language of creation having lived contemporaneously with Shem and Noah. Through Abraham, the biblical story of creation was passed down and maintained. The knowledge of Creation was handed down to the generations exactly as God told Adam, through the Aleph Beht. He was able to pass on an accurate account of the original creation through the Aleph Beht much like the oral tradition of the Native Americans who passed origin stories to their generations. We find proof of this in the book of Job who was a grandson of Abraham who wrote about the original creation, Job Chapters 38, 39. Enoch was not the first author but was called the scribe of God meaning he carried on and maintained the scriptures handed down to him.

It is our assertion that Adam wrote the first book, Genesis 5:1 *"This is the book of the genealogy of Adam. In the day that God created man."* What do you think Adam was doing for thirty some years? YHWH taught Adam the Aleph Beht in the garden; revealing the word by which He created the heavens and the earth. Adam put into practice what God commanded him naming all the animals and keeping an accurate record of them in a book (scroll). Enoch who is the seventh generation of Adam was known as the scribe of God and wrote several books, but he is not the inventor of the Aleph Beht. All of these books were passed to Noah who took them through the flood and taught them to his family including Abraham. The scripture commends Abraham for being faithful to God teaching his descendents the Aleph Beht, the laws and ways of God. The book of Jasher teaches that Abraham spent his first forty years living with Noah and Shem. All of these men were highly educated in the things of God and intricately instructed in the Aleph Beht. They were not crazy men wandering around the wilderness who never took a bath as depicted by Hollywood. Just consider the accuracy and depth of the scriptures. Traditional Christianity teaches that Moses was the inventor of the Aleph Beht even though he had very little contact with his Hebrew roots and was educated in the house of Pharoah.

Moses spent forty years with his father-in-law Jethro who the Bible calls a Priest of God. I don't think that was a mistake. Jethro was a grandson of Abraham and was reared in the tradition of Abraham and had been taught the Aleph Beht by his father and was called the priest of God because he maintained the scriptures. These scriptures were handed down to Moses.

We can trace the tradition Abraham left his descendants through Reuel, Moses' father in-law. Reuel was a son of Esau who was a son of Isaac dwelling in the land of Midian; He was a priest of God. For forty years Reuel passed the Aleph Beht and the traditions of Abraham unto Moses who had been educated in the house of Pharaoh, Moses had little contact with his blood father.

Abram is our model for fathering. The covenant blessing given to Abraham was not only passed on through his descendants, but also gives us the godly model of fathering. Isaac and Ishmael weren't Abraham's only sons, for after Sarah died, he remarried and had many additional sons with his wife Keturah and concubines, "*And she bore him Zimran, Jokshan, Medan, Midian, Ishbak, and Shuah ...*" (Genesis 25:2, 3). Abraham lived one hundred and seventy-five years teaching and training his sons and grandchildren. All of the children were mentored and intricately woven into the culture and traditions of Abram which were centered around the Paleo Aleph Beht. Evenings would be spent together listening to the stories and traditions Abraham had received from Shem and Noah. God recognized his faithfulness and said, "*For I have known him, in order that he may command his children and his household after him, that they keep the way of the Lord* [YHWH] ... " (Genesis 18:19). Before he died, Abraham sent his sons to the countries of the east where they carried his culture as their inheritance, "*But Abraham gave gifts to the sons of the concubines which Abraham had; and while he was still living, he sent them eastward, away from Isaac his son, to the country of the east*" (Genesis 25:6). Isaac alone received the covenant blessing.

The rule of kings came to dominate the nations during Abraham's era, and rule of force by tyrants was the common practice at that time. Genesis chapter 14 gives us a glimpse into Abram's commitment to the governmental model of the "*Family Nation of YHWH*", and his rejection of the "Rule of Force". Kings were continually at war and battled for dominance during this era. Chedorlaomer, the king of Elam who had displaced Nimrod, was dominant in that region and extracted tribute from weaker kings who were subservient to him including Nimrod. Several kings rebelled, including the kings of Sodom and Gomorrah who went out to war against Chedorlaomer and his allied kings—four kings against five. Chedorlaomer's confederacy was victorious over the insurgency, and sacked all of the surrounding cities including Sodom and Gomorrah, taking all of the people including Lot, Abram's nephew. Upon hearing the news Abram mobilized a small army of three hundred and eighteen and mounted a surprise attack on Chedorlaomer's camp by night. Abram's army routed the rouge kings and recovered all of the people who had been taken captive as well as the booty that had been taken.

The Abrahamic Blessing was an actual impartation of national sovereignty and power in both the spiritual dimension and in the natural that gave Abram power over his enemies. This dynamic was confirmed by his military victory over overwhelming odds. According to the customs of the time, Abram had all of the full rights to become the conquering king considering his victory over Chedorlaomer, the former ruling force. Not only in the physical realm was he victorious but also in the spiritual realm the ruling spiritual principality was defeated releasing the dynamics of the Kingdom of God. When Abram returned from defeating the kings, it was expected that he would assume the reign of force. The king of Sodom came out to meet him in a subservient manner, *"Give me the people, but the goods are yours."* Abram objected saying, *"...I have raised my hand to the Lord (YHWH), God Most High* [El Elyon], *the Possessor of heaven and earth, 23that I will take nothing ..."* (Genesis 14:22, 23). Instead of demanding tribute and assuming the "Rule of Force," Abram acknowledged the rule of YHWH and returned all of the booty. Then he worshipped God, glorifying YHWH, and giving tithes of all his possessions to Melchizedek, the king of Salem and priest of Most High Elohim.

Melchizedek, the priest of the Most-High was the king of Salem. The interpretation of his name, *melek* = "king"and *Zedek*= "righteous" interpreted *"King of Righteousness."* He was the King of Salem, meaning = shalom or peace which made him the King of peace and righteousness. Melchizedek's kingdom was from another dimension as Salem was not yet the city of YHWH. The physical location inhabited by the Jebusites would later become Jeru-Salem but was not the realm of Melchizedek. The scripture does not give the geneology of Melchizedek, but we do know he was not a descendant of Abram and not of the Levitical priesthood. Hebrews 7:3 says he, *"without father, without mother, without genealogy, having neither beginning of days nor end of life, but made like the son of God, remains a priest continually."* This description cannot be anyone of human descent, not even Jesus who had a mother and a human genealogy. Spiritual revelation discloses He was not human but a physical manifestation of **Holy Spirit**. As Hebrews says, "*He was made like the Son of God, remains a priest forever*". This description elevates us into revelation of the Holy Trinity and describes the Holy Spirit as being exactly like Jesus and standing in the priestly order of Melchizedek. I call them the triplets because they are co-equal and perfectly resemble each other. Melchizedek is a title and not a name; the title of the eternal priesthood after "the order of Melchizedek", of which Jesus would later join.

He brought bread and wine, symbolic of the body and blood of Jesus, and blessed Abram. The Bible teaches that the lesser is blessed by the greater. Abram acknowledged God by bowing to Melchizedek the Priest of the Most-High, giving him the tithe of all. Abram's confession, "...*I have raised my hand to the Lord (YHWH)*," (Genesis 14:22), symbolized his acknowledgment of the supreme authority and YHWH's ownership of heaven and earth. He rejected the temptation to acquiesce to Satan's "Rule-by-Force" model, and in doing so released the supernatural dominion of the kingdom of God.

Abraham's story parallels Adam's as they were both called to establish a beachhead in the earth from where YHWH could spread His kingdom into all of the earth. From Abram Israel was birthed and the reign of God and His seed carried through the nation of Israel and through His Son Jesus. *"And I bestow upon you* a kingdom, just as my Father bestowed one upon me." (Luke 22:29)

THE KINDOM MODEL

The *Divine Right of Kings* is the model where blood line families believe they rule by God's mandate. Kings believe they represent God; however, this is not YHWH's governmental model. Instead, His original model was "the family," "the

Household of YHWH." We can give credit to the English for instilling the concept of kingdom into the psyche of the modern world. Thinking of kingdoms through the lens of the European mind we imagine the model of monarchs and castles and despots with princes and princesses sitting on a throne, ruling by divine right; this model began with the despot Nimrod. But looking into the Word of God through the lens of YHWH, we see the "family of God ruling and reigning through Jesus Christ." The idea of families or "the household of God" having a direct communal link with God is a concept that YHWH established and passed on to Abraham. The Hebrew definition of *Abraham* is, "father of nations." The model of YHWH ruling over First Nations was practiced by many Native American Tribes who were totally dependent upon the Great Spirit to lead them. Governmental impartations were given by the Holy Spirit through various ceremonies, council fires, and dances. The purpose of ceremony in tribal tradition was to gain the favor and blessings of Creator.

> *Then Abram fell on his face, and God talked with him saying:* [4] *"As for Me, behold, My covenant is with you, and you shall be a father of many nations.* [5] *No longer shall your name be called Abram, but your name shall be Abraham; for I have made you a father of many nations"* (Genesis 17:3-5).

The Kingdom of God is a prominent theme in the New Testament; however, should more correctly be termed "the Kingdom of YHWH." Jesus came preaching the Kingdom of YHWH, and in this context, we can use the model of rule by force because it is by force (dunamis) that the powers of darkness are cast out. *"But if I cast out demons with the finger of God, surely the kingdom of God has come upon you"* (Luke 11:20). Jesus's announcement ended the rule of darkness on the earth and launched His governing authority in the earth. An impartation of national authority was given to Him and a new nation on earth was born. *"...Jesus came to Galilee, preaching the gospel of the kingdom of God (YHWH), and saying, 'the time is fulfilled, and the kingdom of God (YHWH) is at hand ...'"* (Mark 1:14, 15).

The rule-by-force model of kingdom was an idea that infiltrated the minds of the Israelites that resulted in them rejecting the direct rule of YHWH; instead, choosing to have a man rule over them. *"...they said, 'No, but we will have a king over us, ²⁰that we also may be like all the nations...*"(1 Samuel 8:19, 20). YHWH warned Israel that the governmental model of a monarchy would result in them being enslaved with their descendants; nevertheless, they insisted, and He granted them their wish. As the saying goes, *"We do not get the government we want but the government we deserve."* Thus, Israel rejected God: *"... Now make us a king to judge us like all the nations ...⁷And the Lord* [YHWH] *said to Samuel, 'Heed the voice of the people in all that they say to you; for they have not rejected you, but they have rejected Me, that I should not reign over them"*(1 Samuel 8:6, 7).

The rule of monarchs infiltrated the minds of the Israelites and eventually led to the destruction of the kingdoms Israel and of Judah and their dispersion among the nations. Under the rule of kings, they could never attain to the full blessing of God. Modern Christians advocate for the model of ancient Israel kingdoms to return; however, the kingdom of YHWH will be restored but this time to the model of a Father's nurturing His household.

Modern Christian Zionist's infatuation with the democratic State of Israel and are misguided and enamored with a false model. The modern democratic state of Israel has adopted the Babylonian concept of democratic rule and rejects the direct rule of their King Jesus, which was prophesied in the book of Ezekiel *"... Surely I will take the children of Israel from among the nations ... ²²and I will make them one nation in the land, on the mountains of Israel; and one king shall be king over them ...*" (37:21, 22). Democracy is hardly a substitute for the King of kings, and the Knesset can hardly be considered YHWH's representative government on earth. The current government of Israel at its core is Zionism. Please don't misconstrue this as being anti-Israel, because God will restore Israel but under His order. Consider this exortation a nudge in the direction of YHWH's order.

Jesus gave an entirely different model for His followers based on the *oikos* model that will be addressed in detail in another chapter. The role of the *family of YHWH* is to become His agents and bring His spiritual dominion into planet earth (*Thy Kingdom come Thy will be done on earth as it is in heaven)*. God's strategy has never changed from the time He commissioned Adam in the Garden of Eden to when He empowered the First Nations to when He created a new nation through Abraham and now through Jesus and His family. God gave the model of "family" to Abraham, which was the same model given to Adam in the Garden of Eden—a concept totally missed by modern theologians. The father and the family are the model that Abraham followed, and the Father and family is the model Jesus demonstrated. I have spent years studying various church models, and I can find no better prototypical model for the assembly of the saints than YHWH's model of *father and family*.

ISRAEL, THE SEED INCUBATOR

Israel originated from one man, Abram. His seed became a family, a culture, and then many nations, finally culminating in a young virgin girl who conceived by the Holy Spirit and gave birth to the promised Seed. In the redemptive plan of God, the nation of Israel plays a prominent role as the vessel chosen to incubate the promised Seed. A celestial revelation of a woman in childbirth is given in Revelation chapter 12: "*Now a great sign appeared in* heaven: a woman clothed with the sun, with the moon under her feet, and on her head a crown of twelve stars. ²Then being with child, she cried out in labor and in pain to give birth … ⁵And she bore a male Child who was to rule the nations with a rod of iron..." (1, 2, 5). The woman clothed with the sun and giving birth to the man child is symbolically Israel who was created to be the womb that would carry the promised Seed until the time He would be born into to the world.

The great sign in heaven symbolizes the Old Covenant Israel of God; the woman symbolized Israel, the sun, moon Jacob and his wife and the stars represents their sons. Joseph's dream reveals the identity of the woman: "…Look, I have dreamed another dream. And this time, the sun, the moon, and the eleven stars bowed down to me" (Genesis 37:9). She was also the fulfillment of the prophetic word given to Eve; and also, represents the prophecy to the woman in Genesis 3:16, "He would greatly multiply her pain and sorrow in giving birth to the seed." The fulfillment was all the pain and suffering Israel endured throughout her existence simply to give birth to the Seed, "Then being with child, she cried out in labor and in pain to give birth" (Revelation 12:2). The victory of Jesus over the powers of darkness is the fulfillment of the prophetic word, "He shall bruise your head," and His death on the cross is fulfilled by: "you shall bruise His heel."

Another sign appeared in Revelation 12:3, 4 (KJV):

> "And there appeared another wonder in heaven; and behold a great red dragon, having seven heads and ten horns, and seven crowns upon his heads …⁴and the dragon stood before the woman which was ready to be delivered, for to devour her child as soon as it was born."

The dragon has fought the plan of God from the very beginning and has made countless attempts to destroy the Seed. His diabolical plan to defile the seed by corrupting

Israel. His war has always been against the Seed, and he has made countless attempts to destroy the Seed: "...*And the dragon stood before the woman who was ready to be delivered, for to devour her child as soon as it was born*"(Revelation 12:4, KJV). He attempted to destroy the Seed by killing the newborn babies in Egypt and in Bethlehem, but at every attempt failed to destroy the Seed who was coming to crush his head.

Dispensationalists place the defeat of the dragon of Revelation 12 in the future seven-year Great Tribulation, this false premise gives Satan incredible power over sincere but defeated Christians. Several key points in Revelation 12 occur simultaneously with the Man Child being born and caught up to the throne of God which puts the time period of the dragon being cast out of heaven simultaneous with the resurrection of Jesus.

> "...*And her child was caught up to God and His throne ...*
> *⁶Then the woman fled ... ⁷And war broke out in heaven...*
> *⁹and Satan, who deceives the whole world; he was cast to the earth, and his angels were cast out with him ... ¹⁰for the accuser of our brethren, who accused them before our God, day and night, has been cast down*" (Revelation 12:5-10).

When the Man Child is caught up to the throne of God war breaks out in heaven and Michael and his angels cast Satan and his angels out of heaven. There is a huge difference between a futuristic victory and victory at the time of the resurrection, especially when it concerns spiritual warfare. Jesus's triumph over the power's darkness is the foundational basis of believers victorious overcoming life and their authority in spiritual warfare.

The wisdom of YHWH demanded that the Seed be preserved at any cost. God commanded the Israelites, "... *be holy, for I am holy*" (Leviticus 11:45, KJV). God's command for holiness was intended to guard and protect the Seed.

Holiness was His strategy to insulate and shield His DNA within the nation of Israel, in order to protect the pure and holy bloodline. This made it necessary to separate them from the ungodly idolatrous nations of the earth. There could be no intermarriage and no idolatry, which would defile the Seed. This is why the dealings of God in the Old Testament appear to be racist and extremely severe at times. All of Satan's attacks on Israel had one target in mind—to corrupt and destroy the promised Seed.

YHWH's severe dealings with the nations reveal how vital it was for Him to protect His promised Seed and to safeguard the hope of the whole world. When we fail to see the heart of God and understand how essential it was for Him to preserve the Seed, then His wrath and severe commands appear to make Him a mean, terrifying God. When we understand His reason for His harsh actions and why He did what He did, then we perceive the wrath of God as the love of God and salvation for the whole world.

The holiness of God preserved a pure bloodline, but the Dragon was resolute to blemish the DNA of God by exploiting the bloodline and defile the Israelites. The Dragon attempted to defile the Seed of the woman through idolatry. Also referred to as "iniquity," *idolatry* releases curses upon the human race that is passed down from generation to generation. "*...For I, the Lord* [YHWH] *your God, am a jealous God, visiting the iniquity of the fathers upon the children to the third and fourth generations of those who hate me*" (Exodus 20:5). Idolatry directly affects the seed of mankind; however, holiness preserved the purity of the Godly DNA through which all the world would someday be saved. From the beginning, Satan tried to tinker with the seed of mankind, and even today the seed of man is being altered in the name of research and science. We see the days of Noah returning and the human genetics being corrupted through mRNA injections. Once again the enemy is attempting to provoke the wrath of God upon humanity by defiling the original created order of human DNA. Just as it was in the days of Noah, holiness will preserve the human race.

YHWH God was particularly severe on those who committed idolatry; He knew iniquity would unleash curses upon the whole nation and defile the Seed. When the earth opened and swallowed those who had bowed to the golden calf, thousands died. This was a necessary judgment to protect the integrity of the bloodline and to cut off the curse of iniquity. The natural man sees these extreme punishments as acts of a cruel, angry God, but those who are attentive to the heartbeat of God know how far His love will go in order to bring redemption to fallen mankind.

I explained it to one confused man this way: if a person has gangrene in one leg, it is necessary to cut off the leg in order to save the life of the man. "*And if your right hand causes you to sin, cut it off and cast it from you; for it is more profitable for you that one of your members perish, than for your whole body to be cast into hell*" (Matthew 5:30). This man could only see the severity of God's punishment and the destruction of human life, failing to understand that amputation was essential in order to save the whole human family. By failing to deal with iniquity, the plan of redemption would have ended right there, and I suppose the end of the human race and the world.

Through generations and thousands of years Israel suffered and travailed in labor to bring forth the promised Seed, just as God had prophesied. Even though YHWH had taken extraordinary measures to preserve the Seed, the nation of Israel had gone apostate. Israel had dwindled to a few faithful souls, as it is written: "*...I have reserved for Myself seven thousand men who have not bowed the knee to Baal*" (Romans 11:4). God always has a remnant. In spite of Israel's going apostate, God managed to preserve a pure vessel who was worthy to give birth to the promised Seed. But there only needed to be one, the Virgin Mary! She was the culmination of the "*Woman clothed with the Sun and moon,*" a daughter of Abraham, of the household of David. She was a pure virgin. The angel Gabriel announced, "*... Rejoice, highly favored one, the Lord* [YHWH] *is with you; blessed are you among women!*" (Luke 1:28). Why was she highly favored? Not because she was just any woman, but because she was the culmination of all the pain, the suffering, and all of the labor and travail of a nation through thousands of years. All of God's dealings with Israel came down to this woman whose linage had remained pure. Truly, this was the womb God had provided to bear the Seed and the hope of Israel. In Luke 1:42, the Holy Spirit spoke through Elizabeth and said, "*...Blessed are you among women, and blessed is the fruit of your womb!*" Mary responded by saying, "*He has helped His servant Israel* [Mary], *in remembrance of His mercy, [55]As He spoke to our fathers, to Abraham and his seed forever*" (Luke 1:54, 55). Mary was, in effect, symbolic of a nation, Israel, and the mother of the hope of Israel, Yahshua.

CHAPTER 4

THE INSTITUTIONALIZED ENSLAVEMENT CONSPIRACY

THE ENSLAVEMENT OF ISRAEL under Pharoahic rule demonstrates how Satan uses institutional governmental control to reduce free people to slaves and systematically transforms the psyche of sovereign people into that of slaves. This chapter exposes the conspiracy to enslave humanity through Israel's four-hundred-year bondage in Egypt. I will expose Satan's schemes through the Pharoahic governmental system during the four-hundred- year bondage of the children of Israel, compare it to Indian reservation systems, and show how it has evolved into contemporary governmental systems.

Jacob is an Old Testament analogy of postmodern Christianity. Jacob was the possessor of the promises of God, but he never seemed to be able to measure up to the full potential of his inheritance. God promised the patriarchs that He would bless them and their families in the land of their inheritance. Faith was a concept that was difficult for Jacob to attain even though Abraham had demonstrated the principles of faith. "*And he* [Abraham] *believed in the Lord* [YHWH] *and He accounted it to him for righteousness*" (Genesis 15:6). Jacob's weaknesses always provoked him to resort to his own devices for survival. When he was returning to his homeland from Laban, he sent waves of gifts to appease his brother, whom he feared, which demonstrated his lack of faith in God.

So why did Jacob leave his homeland for Egypt? The descendants of Abraham had learned to live by faith under the providence of a benevolent and living God; they were beholden to no man. Israel migrated into Egypt during a time of famine in Canaan and eventually fell into unbearable circumstances. Formerly a prosperous and free people, the sons of Israel were initially welcomed into Egypt as brothers. "*The land of Egypt is before you. Have your father and brothers dwell in the best of the land ...*" (Genesis 47:6). What initially was a blessing turned into captivity meant to enslave them under the rule of a fierce taskmaster.

Before Jacob brought his family into Egypt, he had gained great stature and was a highly respected man. He was independently wealthy, and they were a sovereign people. They were brought into Egypt by Joseph, one of Jacob's sons, who had been elevated to second-in-command over all of Egypt. Because of Joseph, the children of Israel found great favor with Pharaoh and the Egyptians. Pharaoh allotted them a prime fertile reservation in the land of Goshen. During the great famine, Israel was remarkably provided for inside Egypt. The children of Israel prospered in Egypt and became extremely comfortable, living as first-class citizens much like Christians in the world today. Jacob grew old in the land of Egypt and eventually died, always longing to be returned to his homeland.

History recognizes Pharaoh as an archetype of governmental rule characterized by slavery and tyranny. Pharaoh and his system were the tools of Satan. We see the emergence of satanic rule through the headship of Pharoah a powerful God/King. A national treasury was developed and acquisition of property by the government, a system of taxation, government-sponsored religion, a strong military, a system of health care, judicial, law and order, and legalized slavery.

The Pharoahic system gained control and ownership of all the private land in Egypt through Joseph's "Land-for-Food" policies initiated during the great famine. A strong central bank started by Joseph initiated a program to exchange food for private land during the great famine, and land ownership passed from private ownership to governmental ownership (socialism). When the monetary system in Egypt failed, Joseph's domestic policies to feed the multitudes eventually led to the enslavement of the citizenry of Egypt; the people gladly went along, i.e. "You will own nothing and be happy". The government became the provider of all they had need of.

> And Joseph gathered up _all the money_ that was found in the land of Egypt and in the land of Canaan, for the grain which they bought; and Joseph brought the money into Pharaoh's house. [15] So when _the money failed_ in the land of Egypt and in the land of Canaan, all the Egyptians came to Joseph and said, "Give us bread, for why should we die in your presence? For the money has failed." [16] Then Joseph said, "Give your livestock, and I will give you bread for your livestock, if the money is gone." [17] So they brought their livestock to Joseph, and Joseph gave them bread in exchange ... Thus he fed them with bread in exchange for all their livestock that year ... [18] They came to him the next year and said to him, "We will not hide from my lord that our money is gone; my lord also has our herds of livestock. There is nothing left in the sight of my lord but our bodies and our lands"... [20] _Then Joseph bought all the land of Egypt for Pharaoh_; for every man of the Egyptians sold his field, because the famine was severe upon them. _So, the land became Pharaoh's._ [21] And as for the people, _he moved them into the cities_, from one end of the borders of Egypt to the other end ... [25] So they said, "You have saved our lives; let us find favor in the sight of my lord, and _we will be Pharaoh's servants_'" (Genesis 47:14-25).

The Enslavement of a Free People

In the process of time, Joseph, Pharaoh's viceroy or second ruler died, and a new pharaoh came into power. In ancient Egypt, the people believed Pharaoh ruled by divine right; he was a god/king. Pharaoh ruled a strong central government in order to maintain firm control. During the time of this new pharaoh came the emergence of a satanically inspired highly structured government. Once he gained control of all the land and the people, he could now set his sights on destroying the sovereignty of a free people.

Pharaoh's compulsion for control did not originate out of his love for his country; rather, his rule was motivated by fear and jealousy of a free people. He felt his control over the country was threatened. He feared that this free people would ally themselves with his opposition and instigate free thinking and undermine his political control. His jealousy was fueled by observing the prosperity that Israel was experiencing within his country—much like Hitler's fear and hatred of the Jews. He feared their success would influence his people to seek what they had, and his fear prompted him to enact laws and programs to control the flow of ideas.

> But the children of Israel were fruitful and increased abundantly, multiplied and grew exceedingly mighty; and the land was filled with them. *8Now there arose a new king over Egypt, who did not know Joseph. 9And he said to his people, "Look, the people of the children of Israel are more and mightier than we; 10come, let us deal shrewdly with them, lest they multiply, and it happen, in the event of war, that they also join our enemies and fight against us..."* (Exodus 1:7-10).

Pharaoh knew that, in order to accomplish his goals, it would be necessary to introduce propaganda that would brainwash his people into supporting his agenda by instigating racial prejudice, much like the Nazi system. *"...Come, let us deal shrewdly with them ..."* (Exodus 1:10). To do this, he instigated an unfounded fear of the Jews into the populace. *"But the more they afflicted them, the more they multiplied and grew. And they were in dread of the children of Israel."* (Exodus 1:12). He manipulated public opinion in order to develop support for policies that would strip Israel of its faith and reduce them to a culture of dependence. The conspiracy to consolidate Pharaoh's power was directed to:

1. Stop the population growth of the aliens
2. Reduce their political strength and influence
3. Suppress independent thought and free speech
4. Financially profit through the enslavement of Israel

Enslavement came very subtly. As tribal herdsmen and a warrior society, the twelve tribes had developed their own militia and were capable of marshalling a significant army. The traditional occupation of the Israelites of herdsman kept them independently wealthy and capable of defending their own self-interests, much like today's farmers and ranchers. Pharaoh's political agenda enacted policies to diminish their self-defense and to strip Israel of its identity in order to reduce them to a victim's mentality. It began with dependence. Israel was given a "reservation" in Egypt and allowed to prosper on free land, similar to our American Indian reservations. Initially, they were given sufficient grain to live on, were allowed to maintain their livestock, and were even contracted to care for the government herds (government programs). Eventually, Israel began to depend on Pharaoh for their prosperity; they became a domestically dependent people. Eventually, they lost their traditional profession and gave up on their own self-defense. They forgot their heritage of faith and their divine inheritance from the God of Abraham.

Finally, dependence on governmental support induced trauma, and they lost their identity. They forgot how-to walk-in faith with God. They lost their identity of who they were and who God had created them to be as a free people; they began to identify with Pharaoh and the Egyptian culture. They put on Egyptian-style clothing, they took on Egyptian dietary customs, and they took on Egyptian identity. They were no longer Hebrews; they were hybrid Egyptians. They were integrated into Egyptian society, which today is called *assimilation*, or "being absorbed into the melting pot of the larger culture." When Moses encountered the daughters of Jethro, their description of him was that he was an Egyptian. It amazes me to see our Native American young people identify with black culture, Chicano culture, prison culture, white culture, but they never have any idea of their own identity. Christianity has fallen into the same kind of assimilation into western civilization; they have taken on the identity of the nations and have no identity of their own. The unique culture of the kingdom of YHWH has been altered by the church, and now western Christian culture is viewed as the highest form of civilization.

In Egypt, the Israelites, now stripped of their cultural symbols and identity, replace them with the jewelry and symbols of their host country. Satan excels at enslaving free people; the American governmental policy of eradicating the buffalo herds to starve Indians stripped them of their staff of life, and forced starvation treaties. Native Americans who were once great hunting and warrior societies were reduced to beggars, and the introduction of alcohol destroyed their wills, reducing them to dependency. The great Blackfoot chief, Crowfoot (Isapo-Muxika), made this statement about alcohol: "*We are powerless before this evil.*"[15] The practice of destroying cultures has indeed been perfected through the ages.

---

[15] Hugh A. Dempsey, "Dictionary of Canadian Biography," 1982, http:// www. biographi.ca/en/bio/isapo_muxika_11E.html,accessed 17 June 2016.

After depleting the herds of the Israelites, to help fight poverty, the "benevolent" Pharaoh instituted a public works project that would employ every able-bodied man; today we call it "rebuilding infrastructure." His scheme of consolidating more power was to harness the energy, talent, and strength of the Israelites into profit—similar to modern economic and immigration policies that enrich the oligarchy. He hired the men to labor in government work crews. I am sure in the beginning he offered them good wages and convinced them that building the pyramids was a worthwhile project on which to work.

The Israelites were anxious to please Pharaoh for his generosity. The all-compassionate Pharaoh, who knew what the people needed more than they did, took the formerly independent people and put them under taskmasters. Slowly the workload increased. We have evidence in the Bible that he even used Israelites against each other. By integrating the people into low-level governmental and supervisory positions, they traumatized their own. These representatives of the government began to lay down the law. I have seen Indian people serving in bureaucratic positions and on tribal councils, enforcing the will of the government. These governmental hacks are harder on their own people than any white man ever was.

Mind Control Through Trauma

The public works program eventually turned into a forced labor camp—a form of government-induced trauma. Slowly the burdens increased until they were unable to think like free people. Trauma opens the door to anxiety, stress, demonic oppression, substance abuse, and the breakdown of family structure. The Bible says that when Moses went out to see his brethren, he found two of them fighting.

This is reminiscent of the politics and infighting on the reservations. We see the Israelites beginning to oppress one another, squabbling, and infighting. The people's lives were reduced to hardship, bitterness, and victimization. "...I have surely seen the oppression of My people who are in Egypt, and have heard their cry because of their taskmasters, for I know their sorrows" (Exodus 3:7).

On Indian reservations, the people's mindsets have been locked into a poverty mentality trapped in the cycle of a poverty culture. People are unable to make rational decisions under the weight of oppression, and a poverty mentality controls their way of thinking and worldview. The unique Native lifestyle and traditional culture, maintained a direct spiritual connection with the Creator, is both feared and hated by Satan, who has a unique hatred for the Native American people. His goal for over five hundred years has been to break down and destroy the Native American people and their cultures. The United States government and religious community has conspired in developing westward expansion to destroying the Native community, through governmental control and genocide. This kind of mind- control enslavement comes through the trauma of poverty and violence. It is common for Native people to be locked up in party politics, supporting the social engineering that has actually perpetuated their problems. Natives fail to grasp, that under contemporary political control, it is the same thing over and over again. I call that insanity.

Government-induced trauma is a practice perfected on the Indian reservations and has produced generations of Natives suffering from PTSD at the same rate as veterans returning from combat.

A panel of experts has released a lengthy report detailing the extent of the public health issues plaguing American Indian

children who live on tribal land, concluding that these kids'
lives are being "destroyed by relentless violence and trauma."
"Today, a vast majority of American Indian and Alaska
Native children live in communities with alarmingly
high rates of poverty, homelessness, drug abuse, alcoholism,
suicide, and victimization," the report states. "Domestic
violence, sexual assault, and child abuse are widespread.
Continual exposure to violence has a devastating impact
on child development and can have a lasting impact on
basic cognitive, emotional, and neurological functions."[16]

Federal policies and tribal governments have failed to alleviate the societal problems on reservations and, in most cases, have actually aggravated the situation. For example, the boarding school policy of removing children from families in order to educate them inflicted trauma that we continue to suffer the consequences to this day. Forcefully stripping them of their languages and identities left our people scarred and cultures devastated. These types of policies have perpetuated the cycle of poverty in control of reservation economies.

Pharaoh's policy was designed to reduce the population growth of the Israelites since their birth rate far outpaced that of the Egyptians.The roots of prejudice and hatred always work at reducing population. Pharaoh introduced governmental- mandated birth control by instituting policies to destroy every newborn male child in Israel. Through his government health- care system of midwives, he ordered them to kill every baby boy immediately at birth. The midwives, in good conscience, could not carry out the directive, forcing Pharaoh to order the army to go

---

[16] Tara Culp-Pressler,"The Shocking Rates of Violence and Abuse Facing Native American Kids, 18 November, 2014, (http://thinkprogress. org/ health/2014/11/18/3593300/violence-native-american-kids/)., accessed 17 June 2016.

out and kill every male child under the age of two years old. This policy of terror empowered the army to go into the homes of the Israelite families and to forcefully remove their children. This same type of scenario actually happened to Native Americans during the boarding school era when the government forcibly removed their children from their homes. The government was working under the assumption that by educating the children, they would be assimilated, leading to the coining of a dictum by Richard Henry Pratt, the founder of the Native boarding school in Carlisle, Pennsylvania: "*Kill the Indian but save the man.*"[17]

Satan relishes the slaughter of innocents. He is the chief terrorist and a notorious baby killer. He tampers with the seed of man in order to deform and weaken humanity and to mar the image of God in man. From the very beginning, he attempted to destroy the image of God in mankind, and how much better then to destroy YHWH's image before it is ever birthed into this world through abortion and birth control. He hates the image of God in humanity and burns with jealousy toward mankind. Abortion has gained acceptance in repressive governments throughout history and is repeating itself in our generation. The introduction of Covid and forced vaccinations to alter human DNA is a continuation of his war on humanity.

Pharaoh's rule is once again emerging and is about to be re-imposed upon the whole world. In our own country, the same satanically inspired dynamics are repeating themselves in the politics and policies of our government. Indian reservations have been the grand experiment in the development of highly structured government enslavement and today we are seeing the social engineering policies of enslavement creeping into modern society. If Satan is allowed to have his way, the whole world will become like Indian reservations.

---

[17] Alison Owings, *Indian Voices: Listening to Native Americans* (New Brunswick, NJ: Rutgers University Press, 2001), xv.

CHAPTER 5

THE HEAVENLY FAMILY (THE *AGAPEO*)

"Blessed be the God and Father of our Lord Jesus Christ,
who has blessed us with all spiritual blessings in heavenly
places in Christ,
⁴just as He chose us in Him before the foundation of the world,
that we should be holy and without blame before Him in love, ⁵
having predestined us to adoption as sons by Jesus Christ
to Himself,
According to the good pleasure of His will."
(Ephesians 1:3-5)

IN THE MIND OF YHWH, the whole of humanity was predestined to be included in His family; according to Ephesians 1:4,"*...having predestined us to adoption as sons ...*" Paul goes on to say that all humanity was pre-designed to be accepted into His heavenly love fest joined together as the heavenly family inside of the Creator's tipi. The phrase in Ephesians 1:6, "*...accepted in the Beloved,*" is the Greek word, *Agapeo,* a divine revelation of the heavenly love fest. Who is the beloved? The Greek word, *Agapeo,* is translated in the King James as "the Beloved" (notice *Beloved* is capitalized), but should more correctly be translated as "*the heavenly love fest.*" Which we can conclude to be the Godhead, of the Father, Son, and Holy

Spirit, together with their family. The apostle Paul explains that believers have been "...*accepted in the Beloved*" (Ephesians 1:6), or, God's children have been accepted into the heavenly love fest, inside our Father's teepee.

> *The disciples said to Jesus, "Tell us how our end will be?" Jesus said, "Have you discovered, then, the beginning, that you look for the end? For where the beginning is, there will the end be. Blessed is he who will take his place in the beginning, he will know the end and will not experience death." (The Gospel of Thomas, v. 18).*

When Indians tell traditional stories they begin by saying, "*Long time ago.*" To take our place in the beginning, we must allow the Holy Spirit to take us into eternity past before the earth was created within the inner chambers of the heart and mind of the Godhead. There we find the Holy Trinity bound together, eternal, inseparable, of one substance, and in the manifold wisdom of the One. There they are intricately bound together by the agape love that holds them in one embrace, united and inseparable. To fully comprehend the eternal purpose of God, Jesus admonishes the believer to go back to the beginning to understand the Creator's full intent for the creation of humanity and planet Earth.

Long time ago in eternity past, the *Agapeo* gathered around a council fire. During this council fire, they made their determination to create an intelligent being in their image that possessed the free will to make a rational decision to become a part of the heavenly family. The teepee of the Native Americans gives us a glimpse into the heavenly love fest. Inside the teepee, there is warmth and acceptance and protection. Inside the teepee, there is everything needed to nurture and to rear a family. During this council fire, the Agapeo made the plan to invite mankind into the heavenly teepee. This company of sons and daughters joined together with the Godhead would complete the Heavenly family for eternity. YHWH God's intention from before the beginning of time was to have a family of sons and daughters who would play a part with the Godhead. *"Therefore, come out from among them and be separate, says the Lord* [YHWH]. *Do not touch what is unclean, and I will receive you. ¹⁸I will be a Father to you, and you shall be My sons and daughters, says the Lord* [YHWH] *Almighty"* (2 Corinthians 6:17, 18).

During the council fire, the *Agapeo* unveiled their hidden desire revealed through YHWH's prophetic description of Adam: *"...It is not good that man should be alone; I will make him a helper comparable to him"* (Genesis 2:18). In this statement, YHWH uses Adam to divulge His own secret longing. Yes, YHWH God does have a desire! If we can speculate on the conversation that went on during the heavenly council;

> *Jesus asked Father God, "My Father, what is your deepest desire?"*
>
> *Father God replied, "It is not good for God to be alone. My greatest desire is to have a family, a company of sons and daughters to work with me in my heavenly kingdom. My Son, tell me what is the deepest desire of your heart?"*
>
> *Jesus responded, "The deepest desire of My heart is to have a bride, an intimate companion that is comparable to me."*
>
> *Father turned His attention to the Holy Spirit and asked Him, "Eliyah (Holy Spirit), what is the longing In Your heart?"*
>
> *Eliyah (Holy Spirit) answered, "O Father, My greatest longing is to have a teepee, a dwelling place where I am welcomed, and I can dwell."*
>
> *In the wisdom of the ONE, the plan to create mankind was formulated: "Let us create a being in our own image*

and in our likeness that will satisfy the longing within each Person within the Agapeo … according to the good pleasure of His will, (Ephesians 1:5).

Redeemed mankind satisfies all of the desires of God and reflects the image of the triune Godhead; mankind is a son of God, mankind is the bride of Christ, and mankind is the dwelling place of the Holy Spirit. This marvelous creation reveals the mystery of the Godhead and the simplicity of the holy Trinity; there is one God, and He is a Father, He is a Son, and He is a Holy Spirit. Just like me, I am one, and I am a father, I am a son, and I am a husband.

"Oh, the depth of the riches both of the wisdom and knowledge of God! How unsearchable are His judgments and His ways past finding out! [34]For who has known the mind of the Lord [YHWH]? Or who has become His counselor? [35]Or who has first given to Him, and it shall be repaid to him? [36]For of Him and through Him and to Him are all things, to who be glory forever. Amen" (Romans 11:33–36).

The Apostle Paul when caught up into the third heaven was taught unspeakable mysteries (1 Corinthians 12). The Apostle reveals the mysteries given to him during his third heaven encounter in the book of Ephesians and Colossians. Paul lays out the thesis of his heavenly encounter in the first chapter of Ephesians, from which I have taken the liberty to paraphrase verse 10 as follows:

"In the comprehensive administration of YHWH's household, He is gathering a company of Sons into His heavenly family to complete His eternal purpose on planet earth through the redemptive life of Yahshua HaMashiak" (Ephesians 1:10, interpretation mine).

A NEW MODEL

"That which we have seen and heard we declare
o you, that you also may have fellowship with us;
and truly our fellowship is with the Father
and with His Son Jesus Christ."
(1 John 1:3)

This new model of the heavenly family is articulated in the original Greek by the word *oikos*. The *oikos* is "a primary doctrinal theme in the Bible that needs to be recovered but has been obscured and supplanted by the fraudulent founding of the church. The *oikos* concept of the heavenly family should reform the model of the western church into the model of the Heavenly Family. The "church" is a counterfeit of what YHWH intended; it was formulated to be a substitute to divert believers away from embracing the model of YHWH's family. The institution of the church cannot produce the sons of YHWH. An institution cannot produce sons as it does not have the Seed of YHWH within it; only fathers and a families can produce sons. The model of the heavenly family will come more into focus as we draw near to the return of the Jesus. As we draw near to His return, the ministry of the Holy Spirit will turn the hearts of God's people back to the fathers and family model as prophesied in the last verses of the Old Testament, *"Behold, I will send you Elijah the prophet before the coming of the great and dreadful day of the Lord* [YHWH]. *⁶And He will turn the hearts of the fathers to the children, and the hearts of the children to their fathers, lest I come and strike the earth with a curse"* (Malachi 4:5, 6).

The Greek word *oikos* means "household or family" and is an essential theme in the New Testament, but has been lost or covered up by the dogma of the Pharisees and Sadducees. The Greek o*ikos*, or *family*, is a major theme throughout the Bible that believers must reclaim in order to truly capture YHWH's intent for His people. The conception of a counterfeit we call the "church" has obscured God's original intention. The "church" is the antithesis of the *oikos*, or the "heavenly family." The church exalts man as the head and exerts control over its members. *Oikos* is the family of our Heavenly Father, and the bond that holds it together is much stronger; it is His dwelling place and is held together by a love relationship.

> *"Now, therefore, you are no longer strangers and foreigners, but fellow citizens with the saints and members of the household [oikos] of God ...²¹in whom the whole building [family] being fitted together [intricately intertwined], grows unto a holy temple [dwelling place] in the Lord, ²²In whom you also are being built [knitted] together for a dwelling place of God in the Spirit" (Ephesians 2:19-21).*

The institution called the "church" is a created fiction of mankind—an idol, an illusion, an image that was substituted in place of God's model. The King James Version and most English versions translate the Greek phrase in Matthew 16:18, *"oikodome mou ekklesia,"* as, *"I will build my church."* The English mistranslated the Greek word *oikodome* as "I will build" and mistranslated the Greek word *mou ekklesia* as "My church." The English version conveys the idea of some type of organization or a building construction. This foundational doctrine was a fundamental error and an erroneous prototype that resulted in the failed model of the church and has resulted in innumerable denominations.

The original Greek word interpreted, *eulesia* is, "called-out ones," used approximately 115 times in the New Testament but wrongly translated as "church" in nearly every instance. In fact, the Catholic church uses this verse as its cornerstone to claim supremacy as the universal church. *Oikodome* is composed of two Greek words: *oikos and domé.*

The word *oikos* should be translated as "household or family," and the word *domé* is, "a dwelling place." The phrase *oikodome* should instead be translated as *"build my family household,"* and the Greek word *ecclesia* should be translated as *"called-out ones."* The model envisioned by God is conveyed in my interpretation of *oikodome mou ecclesia*: *"On this rock I will establish my household of called-out ones, and the gates of hell shall not prevail against it."*

God is more interested in establishing His household than He is in building mega-churches, or denominations. It is no wonder so many Christians have an inaccurate philosophy of religion and have become ziggurat builders instead of becoming the sons of God. The first thing Christians do after becoming a congregation is to start a building fund. As a person travels throughout the world skeletons of empty cathedrals and temples stand littered across cities and villages. With this kind of ziggurat-builder mentality, we can see how the Enemy has gained the upper hand in spiritual warfare and has blinded the Western-thinking church.

In fact, the Greek word *oikos* and its variations are prominently used throughout the New Testament; for example, Ephesians 2:21 (KJV), *"In whom all the building fitly framed together groweth unto a holy temple in the Lord,"* leaves the reader with the impression of a castle or a temple, when, in fact, the word *building* is the same word Jesus used in Matthew 16:18, *oikodome* and should more accurately be translated as *"the family or household."* A more accurate translation would be: *"In whom all the family of God closely intertwined becomes His dwelling place through the Spirit."* Jesus used the word *oikos* to describe His Father's house in John 14:2, *"In my Father's house* [oikos] *are many mansions."* In 1 Peter 2:5, *"You also, as living stones, are being built up a spiritual house* [oikos]." Should more accurately be, *"... are built up a spiritual household, or family."* These scriptures are only a few examples of how the English translations have omitted the concept of the family of God and have left us with the mindset of ziggurats and religious institutions.

This concept of the family of God is revealed in the very first letter of the Bible, Breshiyth, the Beht being the first letter represent the household of God. In the Paleo Hebrew letter Beyt we are given the pictorial of a tent or a house. The Paleo interpretation of Beht is that of a family dwelling within the house.

In Native American imagery, the prophetic symbolism of the *oikos* (the family of God) is revealed in the Indian camp and the teepee. In John 14:2 Jesus says, *"In My Father's house* [oikos] *are many mansions* [dwelling places] ..." A better interpretation symbolized by the Indian camp: "In My Father's camp is many tepees." Jesus said, "And if *I go and prepare a place for you ... that where I am there, you may be also"* (John 14:3). This verse has been misinterpreted by many preachers in their attempts to convince parishioners of their mansion in heaven; however, the imagery used by Jesus is present tense and welcomes believers into our Father's dwelling place. There is a place reserved for each one of us in our Father's teepee.

"teepee village"

Our heavenly Father warmly invites us to become a part of His camp and His teepee. In His tepee we find love, acceptance and sustenance, completion; everything is provided.

As a youth, I remember at one of our tribal powwows and being invited into an elder's teepee. Our tradition is to respect the sovereignty of the teepee; you did not enter without being invited. I remember an old lady inviting me into her teepee and warmly welcoming me to participate with her family. She said, *"Come in, you are welcome. If you are hungry, we have food. If you are tired, you can rest. If it is too hot outside, come in and cool off."* I was overwhelmed by her generosity and acceptance I felt. In our Father's camp, we are all welcomed in to the *Agapeo* or "heavenly love fest."

We are not orphans but sons and daughters; in the heart of God, we are counted as His. I was working on my sister's house on the rez with my brother, and our conversation turned to the number of children and grandchildren each of our twelve siblings had. My wife and I had recently taken a set of newborn twins into our home and were in the process of adopting them. I modestly said, "Well, I have five kids."

He responded, "Well, those two don't count."

His words were like a knife stabbing me through the heart. I had just spent the last three years getting up several times a night, praying my little boy through grand mal seizures, and I had developed a protective and intimate bond with him and his twin sister. His statement, *"They don't count!"* echoed in my heart over the next few months.

The Holy Spirit poured His love into my broken heart as I came to understand that most people, Christians and seekers alike, suffer from an orphan's spirit. They feel they don't belong and they don't count; they suffer from a spirit of rejection. The church has left us with the feeling that if we are not members, then we are on the outside. This perception has left millions of people hurt and spiritually orphaned. The American church has perpetuated a model of exclusivity, which has left half of its membership disillusioned. The concept of the church is pressure and conformance. The concept of the heavenly family is welcoming and accepting. Our Father's arms are open and warm as He receives us into His heavenly embrace.

My wife and I have taken these two little ones into our household and have loved them as our own, and as far as we are concerned, they are full members of our family. Fortunately, as my brother became acquainted with our little ones, he fell in love with them. I am happy to report that our adoption went through, and they now officially "count." "*...that we might receive the adoption as sons. ⁶And because you are sons, God has sent forth the Spirit of His Son into your hearts, crying out, 'Abba, Father!'*" (Galatians 4:5, 6).

Indian chiefs were not always selected by heredity, but in most tribes, chiefs were chosen because of their wisdom, their generosity, and their ability to provide for and to protect the camp. Blackfeet camps operated on a spirit of inclusion—not exclusion. In the Blackfeet tradition, we honored such a person with the title of *Ninna* (Blackfeet for "Father") and the title of Chief was never used. Individuals who chose to follow a particular Ninna were free to be a part of his camp; there was no coercion. They were free to go or stay. Indian chiefs were not elected, but chiefs knew they were a chief when someone was following them. Blackfeet Ninnas were fathers to their people.

The picture of life within the teepee is a picture of the family of YHWH. As you go through the door and enter the Father's teepee, the most prominent figure you see is the *Ninna*, sitting on his willow chair directly on the other side of the fire—much like the High Priest who went into the Holy of Holies once a year with fire on the altar of incense. The *Ninna* or "Father" presided over his domain. His chair, the father's throne, is constructed of willow and bound with sinew. It is his place of honor as the head man and head of the family; all activity is aimed at pleasing him. Behind his chair, he hangs his weapons and shield; his other important possessions hang on a willow tripod. He is the provider, the protector, the priest, the lawgiver and king of his domain. His teepee is the dwelling place for his family, and everything is geared toward providing for, protecting, and rearing his family. From his place of honor, the *Ninna* imparts his wisdom and nurtures his family with cultural stories and traditions. On the fire is plenty of food—provision for the whole family. You are given a place to join in fellowship. This picture of the heavenly family dwelling together, intricately woven and edifying one another in agape love is the story of the Bible and the revelation of the mystery of the heavenly family.

> In my Father's camp are many teepees ... I go to prepare
> a place for you beside me, and if I go and prepare a place
> for you, I will come again and receive you to Myself; that
> where I am, there you may be also, sitting next to me
> by the fire. (John 14:2-3, interpretation mine).

"Council Teepee"

The original intent of God was for you to have an exclusive relationship with Him as Father. YHWH placed within your DNA the innate desire to worship and connect with Him. You are not complete until the Godhead has taken up residency within your inner man, and you are connected to the heavenly *Agapeo*. The *Agapeo* is not complete until you have been reconciled to the heavenly family. The *oikos* model of the heavenly family is not complete without believers' reconciliation with "the Father." It is the believer's intimate connection with the Father through worship, surrender and the indwelling Spirit that completes them as human beings and restores them to their place in the heavenly *Agapeo*. *"For you did not receive the spirit of bondage again to fear, but you received the Spirit of adoption by whom we cry out, 'Abba, Father'"* (Romans 8:15).

CHAPTER 6

FROM THE CHURCH TO THE *OIKOS*

"The church today is not going to be revitalized through
efforts to renew, rectify and restore.
The only hope for the church is to become an entirely new
entity through the forsaking
of everything it has embraced that fails to reflect the truth, power, and
essence of Christ's life. It will have to rediscover its true
calling and purpose of God.
It will have to be willing to reform itself into whatever configuration
will enable it to function according to biblical mandates".[18]

THE CHURCH MUST AWAKEN to the fact that the Enemy
has claimed the upper hand in spiritual warfare. It has been a
long process of deception and enslavement that has come down
through the ages, as Jesus said, *"A little leaven leavens the whole
lump"* (Galatians 5:9). By the third century, the organic body
of the Early Church of the first and second centuries began to be
organized under bishops; the Early Church had transitioned from
a dynamic Holy-Spirit-baptized body into a more formal

---

[18] Dr. F. Stoner Clark, "Is Church Renewal a Viable Option?" His Presence on
Line: Preparing the Church for the Second Coming of Christ, 8 March
2015, *In His Presence.com*, http://hispresenceonline.org/the-end-times/ church-
renewal-pipe-dream-or-viable-option-2/, accessed 16 June 2016.

paternal organization. With the dramatic conversion of the Roman Emperor Constantine in the forth century and the legalization of Christianity, the need for unity and a consistent doctrine motivated church leaders to convene a series of conventions. Through these conferences, the melding of church and state developed as church fathers walked the tightrope of either honoring the emperor or glorifying the risen King. During these councils, the modern Bible was canonized, and a formalized church and religion were unofficially canonized. The spiritual fabric of Babylon was woven into the DNA of the church.

The Dark Ages of the Roman Catholic Church dominated Christianity for hundreds of years until the fifteenth century when a German priest named Martin Luther rebelled against the vassalage of the Roman Church. Luther proclaimed that salvation came through faith alone, apart from belonging to the church. His revelation and the birth of Protestantism brought a flicker of light back into Christianity. However, the problem with Luther's reformation was that they brought the DNA of the Babylonian church into Protestant churches. The message changed, but the corrupt DNA of Babylon was woven into the psyche of the institutionalized church. The pattern and scheme of control by the church remained. Modern churches preach salvation yet perpetuate the form of the apostate church. The episcopal system of Catholicism and the apostolic control of modern churches remain the same and will surely bring the judgment of YHWH upon them.

We are now living in the postmodern era and even reformed and charismatic churches has been co-opted by the government/religious complex and rendered impotent in spiritual warfare. Is it any wonder churches have lost almost half of their membership in the last decade? The problem we are experiencing is attempting to build on a failed model called the church, and far too many good, sincere ministers have been worn out because of the ineffectiveness of their warfare. The article, "Why Do So Many Pastors Leave the Ministry?" states "50% of the ministers starting out will not last 5 years. 1 out of every 10 ministers will actually retire as a minister in some form. And 4,000 new churches begin each year while 7,000 churches close."[19] The sin of today's church is ordaining priests, apostles and ministers who are not called and ordained by God. The Sin of Jeroboam was his appointment of priests who were not Levitical and of the linage of Aaron. No wonder the Enemy has infiltrated and gained ownership of the church of today.

I am excited and looking forward to YHWH's family forming into a cohesive body in the near future. When a believer's spiritual senses are opened, and they realize the church is a failed model and start building the *family of God*," then we will see the victorious body of Christ emerge, "*... Extol Him who rides on the clouds, By His name YAH, and rejoice before Him, *5a father of the fatherless ...*6God sets the solitary in families ...*" (Psalm 68:4-6). Unfortunately, for this transformation to happen, many will have to become disillusioned with the failed model and discern God's judgment upon the church. Unfortunately, it will require much persecution. In his book, *The Remnant*, Larry Stockstill identifies the same problem yet continues to hope that the church will somehow reform itself. *"It seems to me that the primary reason for ministerial instability and failure, and the first dysfunction in many churches, is a lack of fathering. Mentoring and fathering, is a basic human need, and no Christian is exempt from it.*"[20] What Stockstill fails to understand is that fathering

---

[19]   Bo Lane, "Why Do So Many Pastors Leave the Ministry? The Facts Will Shock You," Expastors.com, 2012-2015, http://www.expastors. com/why-do-so-many-pastors-leave-the-ministry-the-facts-will- shock-you/, accessed 17 June 2016.

[20]   Larry Stockstill, *The Remnant: Restoring Integrity to American Ministry* (Lake Mary, Fla.: Charisma House, 2008), 3.

cannot be sustained in a model that is not the family of God. Institutions cannot produce fathers and sons; only families produce fathers and sons!

The *oikos* model of the "called-out ones" *(ecclesia)* can only be propagated by fathers and sons. This concept is organic and difficult for the control mindset to adjust to. Keep in mind that when I am referring to fathers and sons, I am speaking on a spiritual level. Through my years of ministry, I have developed a father-and-son relationship with many converts, and I enjoy an affectionate relationship with them. Our relationships must be as committed to each other as blood families, with unconditional love being the glue that holds it together. We must be just as concerned with the well- being of our spiritual children as we are our natural. We must also understand that "sons of God" is a not *gender* specific. God's family has no male and female; we are all children and, if children, then heirs. *"The Spirit Himself bears witness with our spirit that we are children of God, and if children, then heirs— heirs of God and joint heirs with Christ..."* (Romans 8:16, 17).

The obvious question that arises: *"Brother Lockley, are you just a bitter Christian? You can't just throw the baby out with the bathwater."* For most of my years in ministry, I was the greatest advocate of the church. My observations and opinions on the church have come from forty years of pastoring, decades of experience, thousands of hours of prayer and study, much sacrifice and suffering, and a sincere desire to seek first the kingdom of God. I experienced success, failure, fulfillment and disappointment as a pastor, and I portrayed the life of a victorious man of God to those I ministered to. However, I have always been troubled watching church members struggle and suffer while hoping for the promises of God I have watched them run from one revival to another, hoping that the man of God had some kind of magic if he would simply lay hands on them. I have watched Satan gain the upper hand in people's lives and the ineffectiveness of the church to meet the needs. Some have even died waiting. My conscience was telling me, *something is missing; there must be more.*

As a Pentecostal pastor, I learned to preach all of the remedies but was never fully satisfied with the results. How many times have we cried for unity and called the churches together in "Unity Gatherings" only to have them go back to their sectarian ways? How many inner healing and spiritual warfare conferences have we attended just to have to go back and do it all again at the next fad movement? For a person to be set free from the mind control of religion and the pressure to conform, he must become emotionally detached in order to make a truthful assessment. In order to do that, the person must become a son of YHWH, and He has the capacity to set the captive free of Babylon. As my German pastor-friend said, "*There must be more!*"

Jesus made this famous proclamation in Matthew 16:16, 18: "*...You are the Christ, the Son of the living God.*"...[18]*And I also say to you ... on this rock I will build My church, and the gates of Hades shall not prevail against it.*" These verses contain the essence of the plan of God but have been spun into an illusion and have been exploited by western Christian denominations. The essential truth has been altered, which has allowed the Enemy to gain the upper hand. These verses clearly epitomize the victorious family of YHWH built on an intimate relationship with Jesus Christ through the Holy Spirit with victory over all of the powers of the Enemy. Catholicism has been the major offender; however, many apostolic leaders have misrepresented Jesus' declaration by attributing the promise to the church. The misinterpretations of this portion of scripture have resulted in the genesis and founding of the idol called— "the Church."

The actual proclamation made by the apostle Peter had two themes: 1) "Thou art the Christ (Messiah or King), and 2) The Son of the living God." The dual aspect within this verse is missed by many: first revelation that Jesus the Messiah will establish YHWH's government on the earth and secondly the humanity in His sonship. Catholicism teaches that this portion of scripture is the appointment of Peter as the "rock" and the hierarchal descendancy of the Roman Catholic popes and clergy. I remember when I first got saved; my family called a meeting with the Catholic priest. I was a brand-new Christian and didn't know anything.

The priest challenged me with this question: "By whose authority do you perform the Eucharist?"

I replied, "By God's! By whose authority do you do the Eucharist?"

He replied, "By the authority passed down from the Apostle Peter."

The perversion of these verses has been exploited by Babylonian religion and used to subjugate millions down through the centuries, with over a billion adherents today.

The first revelation is Jesus as Messiah, the King of Zion, presents the believer with His authority and national dispensation to found the Kingdom of YHWH in earth; the second is Jesus' humanity as the Son of God presents the believer with identity; that we as humans can be a part of His family. Jesus is a resurrected human in a glorified body, and, while on earth demonstrated His relationship with God as Father. Jesus declared, *"... and upon this rock I will build my church"* (Matthew 16:18, KJV); the rock referring to Mount Hermon from where the Gates of Hell were released, and the Holy Spirit's revealing Jesus the Messiah the Son of YHWH building his army and conquering the Gates of hell, *"Now, it shall come to pass In the latter days that the mountain of YHWH's house, Shall be established on the top of the mountains."* (Isaiah 2:2). Established on top means the Gates of Hell have been put under our feet!

The Sons of YHWH are built upon Mount Zion victorious over the rock, and coming into the reality of the promise: *"...the gates of hell shall not prevail against it"* (Matthew 16:18).

The degree to which these truths are opened to the believer reflects his level of maturity in sonship. Out of the believer's revelation of the Kingship of Jesus and as co-heirs and sons of YHWH, the Holy Spirit is nurturing a family of warriors called out of the world who will demolish the gates of hell: "... *Till I make Your enemies Your footstool*" (Psalm 110:1).

The ramifications of the promise are played out on three levels: firstly, "...*the gates of Hell shall not prevail against it*"; secondly, "... *I will give you the keys of the kingdom*"; and thirdly, "*whatever you lock up on earth is locked up in heaven, and whatever you loose on earth will be loosed in heaven*" (Matthew 16:18, 19, interpretation mine). The Sons of YHWH are given the keys, or authority, to establish YHWH's kingdom and to establish a new culture from heaven, which involves releasing the dynamics of the kingdom of God and conquering entrenched and institutional demonic hierarchies and the Gates of Hell that were released from on top of Mount Hermon to destroy humanity, (Enoch 6).

The old King James Version uses the term "*to bind*." I remember spending hours upon hours, and prayer meeting after prayer meeting binding spirits. I certainly had faith to do it, but looking back I see that for all of the effort there were very few results. The Greek word, *bind (deo)*, could be defined "to lock up." "*Whatever they lock up on earth is locked up in heaven, and whatever they unlock on earth shall be opened in heaven*" (interpretation mine). The authority to use the *keys of the kingdom* sets apart the spiritual authority of the sons of YHWH, not only in the sense of having authority to use the keys in spiritual warfare but also in unlocking the provisions and power of the Kingdom of YHWH on earth. Using the keys to lock up the powers of darkness enforces kingdom authority that binds demonic spirits to the judgment already passed upon them from two thousand years ago at the cross of Calvary. This dynamic should be demonstrated in our communities.

The spiritual authority of the sons of God is comparable to the rod given to Moses at the burning bush, which served as God's implement to release kingdom authority. The keys to bind are used to expel demon spirits, and to apply the judgment that was passed on them and to drive them back to the pits of hell. The keys to unlock opens the doors to the promises and provisions of God and releases spiritual dynamics into physical realms. This verse in Mark 11:22 brings the believer into the authority they possess in spiritual warfare as the mountain refers to Mount Hermon and the removal of the Gates of Hell that were released from there (Enoch 6).

> "... Have faith in God. ²³For assuredly, I say to you, whoever says to this mountain, 'Be removed and be cast into the sea,' and does not doubt in his heart, but believes that those things he says will be done, he will have whatever he says. ²⁴Therefore I say to you, whatever things you ask when you pray, believe that you receive them, and you will have them" (Mark 11:22-24).

Every believer is confronted with the choice between two spiritual realities: Mount Zion, the city of the great King, or Mystery Babylon, the mother of harlots. On a superficial level, they have the same appearance, but, in reality, they are the antithesis of each other. For the ordinary believer, it is hard to discern between the two, and Satan has capitalized on his blindness in order to take advantage. The problem is, we have been trying to get God to come into our house (the church), while all the time he has been trying to get us to come into His house (Zion). Those who have ears to hear the voice of God and are led by the Holy Spirit take the narrow path that leads to the holy mountain of YHWH. Jesus dwells in the secret place and while western civilization has programmed humanity to follow the wide road of church and religion, they are taking the path that leads to desolation. The church is a façade—an illusion that

Christianity has wholeheartedly embraced. As a friend of mine, Kevin LaPlante, said, *"In order to see the illusion we must first become disillusioned. Many people who have left the church when asked why will say, 'We got disillusioned with the church.' That is exactly where God wants us; we must become dis-illusioned before we can see the illusion."*

When I was a newborn Christian, one of my all- time favorite preachers was a Crow Indian named Harold Carpenter, a mighty man of God, who never failed to emphasize in his preaching: *"God isn't interested in manmade systems."* The model we have been handed is a cleverly disguised image but, nevertheless, if it is man-made, it is an illusion. I don't care how nice or how big and organized you think your church is; the day of reckoning is coming! It's time for a new model—one that has come out of heaven.

A regular part of my prayer is to release my full inheritance and that of my children. It is important for the believer to know that YHWH has already created and reserved, in His storehouse, everything that you will ever have needed. The prayer of faith releases your invisible inheritance to be manifest in your life. This is not greed because you can only release what God has stored up for you, but YHWH is much more generous than most believers are willing to believe.

Today, a gathering of Christians is known as "having church." *Ecclesia* is the actual Greek word that is used in the New Testament, which originally meant "an assembly called out by the magistrate." It was in that sense the word implied; however, it was co-opted by the interpreters and labeled as "the church." The question is: "Who calls out the Christian assembly?" Modern Christians assume that Sunday is the time to assemble, and the Sunday assembling of people is called church; however, according to kingdom culture, Jesus is the One who is sweetly calling and inviting people to His gathering, *"For where two or three are gathered together in My name, I am there in the midst of them"* (Matthew 18:20). And as can be clearly seen, only two people are needed to be *the gathering together in His name,* which can happen any place and at any time.

The promise of Jesus to be,*"in the midst,"* should be enough to compel hungry believers to break out of the church walls and demand more Jesus. *"He entered Capernaum after some days, and it was heard that He was in the house"* (Mark 2:1). When Jesus is in the house, there is no telling what might happen! It is important to note that we need to be gathered *in His name under His authority.* The *idol* called "the church" was created to worship man and removes the Creator as its head! The modern charismatic institutions we call "the church" are nothing more than the elevation of man above God and the worship of worship. In today's modern church, we have superstar evangelists and worship leaders. We have superstar pastors and bishops, the flock of God idolizing those who are elevated. The Holy Spirit may come and bless those sincerely seeking Him, but the full dynamic of the power of God is missing because believers have elevated a manmade institution into idol status. The Holy Spirit yearns to find those who will worship in spirit and in truth.

"IT IS NOT GOOD FOR GOD TO BE ALONE"

The deepest longing in the Creator's heart is for an intimate relationship with His intelligent, created beings. YHWH exposed his heart's desire through Adam: *"...It is not good that man should be alone ..."* (Genesis 2:18). Prophetically God is saying, *"It is not good for God to be alone"*? Genesis chapter two says that God created Eve to be *equal* to Adam or "comparable" to him for good companionship. Because she is comparable to him, she has the right to choose whether or not to enter into covenant relationship with him or not. First Woman is symbolic of the Bride of Christ who has made herself ready; *"And to her it was granted to be arrayed in fine linen, clean and bright, for the fine linen is the righteous acts of the saints"* (Revelation 19:8). The Creator desires a relationship that is not forced or contrived but one out of a sincere love and the freedom to enter into covenant relationship with Him. One of the coolest examples of the bride's making herself ready is in Blackfeet courtship.

In the Blackfeet Indian camp, the courtship ritual is symbolic of the bride making herself ready. In the camp, marriages were arranged by the families of the couple, but relationships were formed by the young people. When I was a youth, I remember attending the powwows. At the end of an evening of dancing, the drummers would play the "Blanket Dance." This dance was ladies' choice, the girls chose a boy with whom to dance under the blanket. I was a shy boy, but I enjoyed being under the blanket with a girl. As the young people grew older and the young men proved themselves to be capable warriors and good hunters, they became eligible for marriage. The young men would court the girls by hiding where the young ladies gathered and play love songs on their flutes to attract an interested partner; the families would arrange the marriage.

The courtship occurred when the *Ninnas* (fathers), would sit down and discuss an appropriate dowry. A price was agreed upon, depending on how much they valued the bride. The exchange would be made, but the marriage would not take place until the bride made herself ready. In Blackfeet culture, the bride was required to build the wedding teepee, furnish it and make a complete set of regalia for the groom and herself. This task was usually a family effort. The wedding teepee, which was made from eight to twenty-plus buffalo hides, would be set up in the middle of the camp. While the regalia and teepee was being prepared, the bride would impress her future groom by preparing delicious meals, probably boiled buffalo meat with turnips and a good portion of berry soup. Every day, she would walk through the camp in full sight of everyone to deliver the food to her intended groom. Finally, when all of the regalia and furnishings had been completed, she would cook another delicious meal. This time instead of delivering it to her suitor, she would take it to the bridal tent. When the groom got hungry and discovered there was no meal, he would go looking. Inside the wedding teepee everything was prepared! His bride had made herself ready. *"Let us be glad and rejoice, and give honor to Him: for the marriage of the Lamb is come, and his wife hath made herself ready"* (Revelation 19:7).

The universal law of free will is a principle much deeper and more profound than is commonly appreciated, but it is the laws of grace and free will that gives the Bride the freedom to willingly enter into the marriage covenant with her Bridegroom. The Creator knew that in giving man a free will there was the possibility that First Man would fail. In His divine foresight, He knew that in giving man a free will, there was the possibility he would make the wrong choice. If First Man willingly chose to sin, the righteous demands of justice would be invoked and demand to be satisfied. The eternal laws of heaven would condemn him and revoke his standing with God! The claims of justice would demand eternal damnation and eternal separation from the Godhead; *"... the wages of sin is death ..."* (Romans 6:26). The death penalty would be invoked and demand to be paid in full.

During the heavenly powwow, the Agape Council deliberated and considered the consequences of failure, *"If the man sins, the consequences of his actions will demand the death penalty; man's blood must be shed."* A strategic decision was made by the Godhead at that time to set in motion the plan of redemption. Conflicting attributes of God's nature had to be resolved; the righteousness of a holy God demanded justice, whereas, the love of God extended grace and mercy. Jesus stood up and announced, *"If the man sins, I will take his place, I will become his substitute, I will take his sin upon myself, and my blood will pay the penalty!"* At this point in eternity past, Jesus became *"... the Lamb of God, slain from before the foundations of the world"* (John 1:29).

Satan cast a shadow of a doubt in the mind of Adam when he questioned the validity of the death penalty. *"... Has God indeed said, 'You shall not eat of every tree of the garden?' ²And the woman said to the serpent, 'We may eat the fruit of the trees of the garden; ³but of the fruit of the tree which is in the midst of the garden, God has said, 'You shall not eat it, nor shall you touch it, lest you die.' ⁴Then the serpent said to the woman, 'You will not surely die' "* (Genesis 3:1-4). The actual consequences of their actions were much more profound than they realized; in legal terms, Adam committed the first murder when he chose to sin. His willful and adulterous act not only invoked the death penalty but unleashed the claims of justice and condemned Jesus to death.

Nevertheless, the plan of redemption covered all of the bases in case the man failed; it was worth the risk. The willingness of our Father to sacrifice His Son to save mankind, and the willingness of the Son to sacrifice Himself for mankind reveals the grace of God and authenticates the tremendous value they place in mankind. Jesus' selfless sacrifice demonstrated how much this new man they had created was valued, and the importance of their investment in humanity, and the glory of their inheritance in redeemed mankind. *"...that you may know what is the hope of His calling, what are the riches of the glory of His inheritance in the saints"* (Ephesians 1:18).

It was necessary for First Man to wear the mantle of the glory of YHWH God. First Man was created perfect;

he was the template—the original design for all humanity. God clothed all of the other animals with coats of fur and feathers and scales, but First Man was created naked. He was the only created being that was naked. The marvelous coats of furs on the animals were the glory Creator gave to them; however, it was First Man place, in time and in relevance as God's crown jewel of creation to wear the glory of God for his covering. In understanding the kingdom authority of the sons of God this is an important principal. He has given His sons regalia to wear, and in the spiritual dimension we are recognized by our unique clothing and the glory of God.

First Man was not created as an infant but as a full-grown man with all of his faculties. He was a spirit man connected to a body through his soul; existing in both the spiritual and physical dimensions on the earth. First Man had spiritual senses; spirit eyes, spirit ears, a spirit voice, a spirit mind, and light dwelled within his being. The spirit of man was dominant and the body was in submission to the spirit; that, combined with the mantle of the glory of God (the Holy Spirit), man was a spiritual being. Adam lived in this dimension for thirty three and a half years before sin enter in.

God is Spirit. How can you walk with and communicate with a Spirit unless you are spirit? Having eyes opened to the spiritual dimension not only exposed First Man to the reality of the spiritual realm, but in fact, it was Adam's dominant reality. Adam walked with God and talked with God. Adam's perception of YHWH was with his spiritual eye fully exposing God; his third eye was fully opened and developed (I use the term "third eye" in reference to the spirit eye). Whenever God came to Adam in the garden in the cool of the day, Adam fully perceived God, not only with the physical eye but also with the spiritual eye. Yes, the spiritual dimension is more real than the physical material dimension. Mankind has been locked out of the spiritual dimension.

Why did Jesus live for thirty-three and a half years? Because in order to fulfill the requirements of Justice it was necessary for Him to duplicate Adam's life span before the Fall, and experience the full requirement of the penalty. Adam walked with and talked with God or thirty-three and a half years. What do you think he was doing all that time? God educated Adam in the Aleph Beht; He was fully educated. The naming of all of the animals was Adam's Thesis for His diploma. Adam learned the Aleph Beht and passed it on to his family.

"And t*hey heard the sound of the Lord God walking in the garden in the cool of the day, and Adam and his wife hid themselves from the presence of the Lord God*" (Genesis 3:8). The word *presence* specifies a face-to-face relationship. Adam and Eve had a face-to-face relationship with God that challenges the imagination. The Hebrew interpretation of *Eden* indicates that it was "a pleasurable and delightful place"; everything was provided. A couple of thoughts we can consider regarding this verse: first, they heard God walking, and then they hid from His presence, which means there was a spiritual and a material presence. How can one hear a spirit walking? There must have been a physical presence and spiritual presence. So, we can deduct that the relationship was not only in the physical but also in the supernatural realm. Before Adam's rebellion, there was no sin to inhibit the relationship. Adam and Eve heard God walking, but their spiritual eye had already been impaired because the effect of sin caused them to hide their faces from God. Man was locked out of the spiritual dimension and became physical beings.

Before the Fall, First Man's encounter with the serpent who also is a spirit was in the spiritual dimension. Bible scholars and teachers have developed Pharisee doctrines about the serpent being some form of a serpent being that walked on two legs in the physical realm, but after he was cursed, he slithered on his belly. This is erroneous because these scholars do not understand the spiritual dimension, and neither do they understand the "third eye" (spiritual eye). When Eve encountered the serpent, she saw him with the third eye in the spiritual dimension, and she communicated with him in the spiritual dimension—the same way Jesus encountered the tempter in Matthew 4:3-11. "*Now when the tempter came to Him ... But He* [Jesus] *answered ...*" (vv. 1, 2). The serpent Eve encountered is the same serpent mentioned throughout the Bible. He is a spirit. The temptation for Adam was between the spirit and the natural. Because he chose to submit to the natural man, he lost his standing with God. Christians are given the same choice: "*...Walk in the Spirit, and you shall not fulfill the lust of the flesh*" (Galatians 5:16).

It is important for the believer to know that the serpent never had physical legs; but in fact, he is a spirit just like God is spirit (John 4:24). The serpent that Eve encountered in the garden is the same serpent spoken of throughout the Bible. Job chapter one mentions him: "*...From where do you come?*" *So Satan answered the Lord and said, "From going to and fro on the earth, and from walking back and forth on it*" (v. 7) He is also the same serpent referred to in Isaiah 27, Luke 4, Matthew 4:8, and throughout the Old Testament all the way to the book of Revelation. "*So the great dragon was cast out, that serpent of old, called the Devil and Satan, who deceives the whole world; he was cast to the earth, and his angels were cast out with him*" (Revelation 12:9). Modern theologians cannot grasp the concept that Adam and Eve were as much, if not more, in tune to the spiritual realm as they were to the physical creation.

When the tempter showed Jesus all the kingdoms of the world, He wasn't seeing the geographic kingdoms of the world; rather, He was looking into the spiritual dimension and seeing the operations of the Gates of Hell. His encounter with Satan was on the same level as was Adam's. Satan took Him to the top of Mount Hermon and declared, *"All this authority has been given to me and I give it to whoever I wish"* If God were to open our eyes to the spiritual dimension, the sight would scare us to death. However, it is vital for believers to seek the restoration of all spiritual senses in order to take their place as the sons of God and to experience God on the same level or greater than First Man.

CHAPTER 7

THE SPIRITUAL REALM

Behold, what manner of love the Father has bestowed on us, that we should be
called sons of God! Therefore, the
world does not know us,
because it did not know Him. ²Beloved, now we are sons
of God; and it has
not yet been revealed what we shall be, but we know
that when He is revealed,
we shall be like Him, for we shall see Him as He is.
(1 John 3:1, 2)

FOR THOSE WHO TRULY love God and are faithful to him, these are the best of times. In the coming days, those seekers who have been *built upon Mount Zion* will be permitted to enter into realms of God that no church of any previous age has walked in. In the midst of this bleak assessment of the church, God has those who are faithful. Down through the ages, God has always had a remnant; it is no different today.

Since the fall of Adam, the spirit dimension has been closed to mankind in order to buffer believers from evil spirits until they become fortified with the Spirit of God. We should be happy we don't see into the spirit realm because of the demons that would frighten and deceive us. To see into the spirit realm is not only to see angels but also to see the other spirits in that realm that are demons. However, as we progress further into the chaos of these end times, we are going to have an *open heaven* as Jesus promised Nathanael in John 1:51, *"... hereafter you will see heaven open, and the angels of God ascending and descending upon the Son of Man."* At the Baptism of Jesus, the spiritual dimension that humanity had been locked out of was opened, *"When He had been baptized, He came up immediately from the water, and behold, the heavens were opened to Him.* (Matthew 3:16). This statement is far more significant than just for casual reading. We have to keep in mind that the heavens had been closed since the time of Adam's sin and only a handful of prophets had been given access to heaven. When the heavens were opened to Jesus, they were also opened for believers to enter. This was a marker and a new epoch of time. Jesus spoke of Nathanael, *"... Behold, an Israelite indeed, in whom is no guile"* (John 1:47). The word *guile* means "deceit." In other words, Jesus was saying that when we are without deceit or any other hidden works of darkness, we will be able to enter into the spirit realm. There can be no areas of hidden darkness within our being as the demons would take advantage of us.

It is important that we understand what is in the spiritual realm and how it operates as we transition from the world, as we have known it, into the new world that will gradually escalate into chaotic changes. God will gradually open to us the reality of the spirit realm that is all around and has been hidden from our sight. The nations of the world are going to be breaking apart in the coming days, and believers must leave Babylon in order to enter into the spiritual kingdom of God. This transition must begin with a deep, abiding relationship with Jesus Christ and a spiritual revelation of what the spiritual realm is like. But as we trust in Him, we know that He will do in us that what He has promised: *"Being confident of this very thing, that He which hath begun a good work in you will perform it until the day of Jesus Christ"* (Philippians 1:6, KJV).

As I have already mentioned, the church has been effectively removed from spiritual authority and cannot do the job YHWH has called His sons to do. As the body of Christ is transitioned from being *the church* to becoming *the family of YHWH,* the spiritual dimension will be opened. Spiritual warfare will become a routine activity for the sons of YHWH.

Spiritual warfare should be a natural part of our daily life as God's children. When we pray, we should be praying in tongues and breaking curses along with our other daily prayers. The Holy Spirit will lead us in this practice. When you suspect someone hates you or is working against you, break curses from them. It could be that their evil thoughts toward you are arrows from Satan's quiver to war against you. Memorize Scriptures about your position in Christ and pray those, Scriptures. As sons of God, we have tremendous power in the spirit realm. The problem is that many of us get locked up in the natural realm, forget we are in a war and fail to use our weapons. The world is a wicked place now and we cannot survive without a spiritual awakening.

The Fall of the human race from its original form was more devastating than we realize. After the Fall, mankind's spiritual senses were closed—exactly the opposite of what the serpent told First Woman, *"For God knows that in the day you eat of it your eyes will be opened, and you will be like God, knowing good and evil"* (Genesis 3:5). In fact, First Man and First Woman were already like God when they were created in His image. In the Genesis account, they *heard* God walking, but the Bible does not say that they *saw* Him; that is because, their spiritual eye was immediately darkened. After the Fall, mankind became prisoners to the natural physical realm and lost all perception of the spiritual dimension. Just like Satan and his angels were locked up in the chains of darkness, man was locked up in the physical dimension, and the spiritual dimension closed. The apostle Paul described it as being *spiritually dead*, or being dead to God: *"… who were dead in trespasses and sins"* (Ephesians 2:1).

The creation of the church was a carefully crafted institution designed to keep believers trapped in the physical dimension. While it offers forgiveness of sins and a born again experience it fails to bring the believer into the full experience of the kingdom dimension. The Apostle John in his gospel described it this way, *"Unless a man is born again, he cannot see the kingdom of God,…(vs 5). unless one is born of water and Spirit, he cannot enter the kingdom of God."* (John 3:3-5). There is a vast difference between seeing the kingdom and entering into the kingdom of God. When one is born again, we are able to see the promises of God in the spiritual realm but for us to enter we must be baptized in the Holy Spirit. We must be born of the Spirit. *"He has delivered us from the power of darkness and has translated us into the kingdom of the Son of His love,"* (Col 2:13). The miracle working power of God is activated through the faith of the believer, the baptism of the Holy Spirit and the resurrection of Jesus and transitions the believer from the prison of the flesh and into spiritual dimension of the kingdom of God.

For spiritual conversion to take place the believer must be transformed by the finished work of Jesus Christ and the Baptism of the Holy Spirit. The Apostle Paul says, *"And when Christ who is our life appears, then you also will appear with Him in glory."* This verse is not just talking about when we get to heaven but the actual appearance of Christ in the believer experiencing and living and walking in the kingdom dimension. Now we are in a position to live and operate as the sons and daughters of God were created for. We become victorious warriors and useful in spiritual warfare.

In developing our spiritual senses, it is helpful for the believer to visualize what is taking place in the spiritual realm. For instance, when I pray for healing, I visualize the demonic oppression that may be in operation at the time. As I pray and I take command in the spirit, and visualize the demon being bound to the judgment passed upon it and fleeing as it is cast out, *"Therefore, submit to God. Resist the devil and he will flee from you"* (James 4:7). The Holy Spirit taught me a helpful lesson one day when I encountered an angry rez dog while I was on a prayer walk. The barking and snarling dog charged me, which would have scared the average hiker, but the Holy Spirit prompted me to take authority over the evil spirit. As I rebuked the demon, the dog instantly fell on his face and ran away yelping. Whenever I pray against the attacks of the Enemy, I picture this dog's falling on its face and running away.

Walking in the Spirit and kingdom dimension allows us to experience the authority and miracle working power of God. On one of my trips to Germany I was invited to minister at a Christian Children's Indian Camp. When we arrived, the camp was being set up and one of the work teams came from a young men's industrial school where several hooligans attended. I being resident evangelist my host asked me, *"Lockley, why don't you go over and preach the gospel to that group of young men?"* I walked over to their area and most of them were lounging around acting bored and they let me know they weren't interested in hearing about Jesus. I stood on an elevated piece of ground and raised my hands and shouted out, *"Listen to me"*, this got their attention. I began to preach Jesus when suddenly a gust of wind came up and a tempest blew down from the west. It was such a sudden storm it actually blew the words out of my mouth. They were all looking at me so I shouted, *"Watch and see the glory of the Lord!"* I raised my hands and commanded the storm, *"Peace be still, I bind every force of the enemy and command you to stop!"* As quickly as the storm came it instantly stopped. The boys were sitting there amazed and I asked them, *"Who of you believe that was just a coincidence or was that of God?"* They couldn't deny it and they all sheepishly said, *"Of Got."* I asked them, *"How many of you will accept Jesus into your life as your Lord and Savior?"* Every one of them raised their hands and prayed.

As the *Agapeo* deliberated, they accepted Jesus' plan to become the substitute for mankind's punishment; they determined, since mankind is locked up in the physical realm, it was necessary for Him to take on the form of a human body. *"And the Word became flesh and dwelt among us, and we beheld His glory, the glory as of the only begotten of the Father, full of grace and truth"* (John 1:14). It was necessary for Jesus to come in the flesh in order to deliver us who were in bondage to the flesh. As a physical man, Jesus paid the penalty that was meant for us. He took our sin upon Himself and became sin for us to deliver us from the devastating consequences of the Fall of the human race. Jesus paid the ransom in full; He paid the full price for our redemption so that we can be restored as the sons of God. *"Inasmuch then as the children have partaken of flesh and blood, He Himself likewise shared in the same ..."* (Hebrews 2:14).

His plan from the beginning was to have a company of warrior sons and daughters, *"For whom He foreknew He also predestined to be conformed to the image of His Son, that He might be the firstborn among many brethren,"* (Romans 8:29).

CHAPTER 8

THE BATTLE FOR PLANET EARTH

"In the beginning God created the heavens and the earth.
² The earth was without form, and void;
and darkness was upon the face of the deep.
And the Spirit of God was hovering
over the face of the waters."
(Genesis 1:1, 2)

IN THIS CHAPTER, I challenge the popular Six-Day Creation theory of many fundamental Christians; I urge my reader not to freak out over my meddling with another sacred cow and consider what I present as it relates to the rest of the story. Throughout church history there have been other biblical interpretations of creation other than the Six-Day theory. In this section, I offer my interpretation which is a modified version of the "Gap Theory." The Gap Theory asserts that there was an unspecified "gap" of time between verses 1 and 2 of Genesis. In the beginning the earth was created perfect; the theory asserts that something catastrophic happened in time past to ruin the original creation or an event marred what had formerly been a pristine and perfect earth.

The first three words of the Bible, *"In the beginning"* do not offer a timeline but take us back to the time of the very beginning of the original creation, which could have entailed millions of years. *"Listen to Me ... ¹³Indeed My hand has laid the foundation of the earth, and My right hand has stretched out the heavens; when I call to them, they stand up together"* (Isaiah 48:12, 13). The first phrase of Genesis 1:2, *"The earth was without form, and void ..."* opens an unspecified epoch of time when a cataclysm devastated the original pristine earth and rendered it *without "form, and void."* Job chapter 38 suggests the possibility that primordial earth had rings: *"Where were you when I laid the foundations of the earth ... ⁹When I made the clouds its garment, and thick darkness its swaddling band,"* (vs. 3, 9). Is it possible that the dust from the thick clouds and the rings settled, covered the earth, creating the fertile soil that brings forth life? Verse three opens to the recreation of planet earth and falls in line with the six-day creation theory.

"In the beginning" (Genesis 1:1) speaks of the creation of the ancient earth sometime in antiquity, which could have been millions of years ago. According to Genesis 1:2, the original created earth *"... became without form, and void; and darkness was upon the face of the deep ..."* The verb *"was"* can be interpreted as *"became,"* i.e., *"The earth became without form and void."* My assertion is that at this time in antiquity, Lucifer and a third of the angels fell from their standing on the mountain of God and were cast into the earth. *"Darkness fell upon the face of the deep..."* (Genesis 1:2, my interpretation), which indicates that Satan and the fallen angels were cast into planet earth and the resulting cataclysm destroyed the original creation. There is a possibility that the fall was accompanied by earth's being struck by an object, possibly an asteroid or other planetary collision. Jesus, who was eyewitness to this horrific event, described it as follows: *"I saw Satan fall like lightning from heaven"* (Luke 10:18), referring to antiquity when Lucifer was cast to the earth.

Jude says, *"And the angels who did not keep their proper domain, but left their own abode, He has reserved in everlasting chains under darkness for the judgment of the great day"* (v. 6).

Jude points out that planet earth is not only a dwelling place for mankind, but is also a prison reserved for Satan and the rebellious angels. The earthly activity and mischief of Satan is described in Job 1:7: God said to Satan, *"... From where do you come?"* Satan replied, *"... From going to and fro on the earth, and from walking back and forth on it."*

Notice in Genesis 1:2, which says, *"The earth was without form, and void; and darkness was on the face of the deep. And the Spirit of God was hovering over the face of the waters,"* there are three levels or surfaces listed in this verse: the earth, the face of the deep, and the face of the waters. Genesis says that darkness was on the face of the deep; this was the abode that was reserved for the prince of darkness and the fallen angels. The second level and the Spirit of God was hovering over the face of the waters, referring to the water that covered the primordial earth. The third level is the earth's surface or the face of the earth which became without form and void as a result of a cataclysmic event that changed the surface of the original planet earth. The original creation suffered catastrophic devastation, possibly at the same time when Lucifer and his angels were cast into the face of the deep, but it was God's intent for planet earth to be inhabited. *"For thus says the Lord* [YHWH], *Who created the heavens, Who is God, Who formed the earth and made it, Who has established it, Who did not create it in vain, Who formed it to be inhabited; I am the Lord* [YHWH], *and there is no other"* (Isaiah 45:18).

In his book, *Planet X: The Sign of the Son of Man, and the End of the Age*, Douglas Elwell explains that the original earth was struck by a moon of "planet X." This moon smashed the earth's crust, gouging out a huge chunk of the earth and thrusting it into space, creating the moon. The six-day recreation begins at verse 3.

I am not a scientist or a geologist, but common sense tells me that something horrific happened to earth at some time in the past. Science has confirmed events, such as the meteorite strike that created the Chicxulub Crater near the Yucatan Peninsula, which allegedly destroyed the dinosaurs. In the state of Oregon, I have preached at Pulpit Rock. This interesting piece of geology has caused me to wonder what could have possibly happened to earth to expel such a huge piece of lava some fifty miles through the air, far enough for it to cool, and land with the point facing down. What could have happened to cause the mountains to be thrust up through the earth's crust for some 28,000 feet and for gorges to open in the surface of the earth some 36,000 feet into the depths of the ocean at the Mariana's Trench? I believe it had to be a sudden catastrophic event that separated the original continent, Pangaea, and formed much of the earth's surface as we know it today. If we attribute the change to continental drift or shifting plates, then why are new mountain ranges not being formed today? Why are the continents not shifting? Is it not possible for God to use a planetary object in His work of creation?

> One very large impact, known as the Chicxulub crater in the Yucatan region of Mexico was large enough all by itself that scientists have surmised that its damage could have rendered the world of the dinosaurs extinct. When the original earth was destroyed, its dry land (Job 38:8-11) was immersed in a global flood, and the earth's surface was darkened. What the Bible may be describing in Genesis 1:2 was something akin to a "nuclear winter," which existed in the aftermath of the annihilation of the dinosaurs and all physical life on the earth's surface.[21]

---

[21]   Steven Collins, "The United States of America in Biblical Prophecy," 2009, stevenmcollins.com/html/usa._in_prophecy.html, accessed 18 June 2016.

If you consider the devastation to planet earth that occurred when Lucifer and his angels were cast into earth, combined with the devastating collision with another planetary form, this earth had to have been drastically changed from its original form. With the defilement that came with the fall of Satan and his angels and the curse that Adam brought on the earth comes a planet in desperate need of healing. According to Romans chapter eight God is going to bring healing and restoration to all of creation (or as the Native Americans believe, "The buffalo and the ancestors will return"). *"Because the creation itself also will be delivered from the bondage of corruption into the glorious liberty of the children of God"* (v. 21). *"For the earnest expectation of the creation eagerly waits for the revealing of the sons of God"* (v. 19). When the precious blood of Jesus was splattered all over the earth at Mount Calvary, the price of redemption was paid—not only for mankind but also for the whole earth!

"The Fall" that Jesus mentioned in Luke 10:18, which says, *"…I saw Satan fall like lightning from heaven,"* occurred when Lucifer, the anointed cherub, exalted himself, took a third of the angels and tried to overthrow God on the mountain of God. In Isaiah fourteen Satan exposed his covetousness in his five "I will":

- *I will ascend into heaven.*
- *I will exalt my throne above the stars of God.*
- *I will also sit on the mount of the congregation on the farthest sides of the north.*
- *I will ascend above the heights of the clouds.*
- *I will be like the Most High.*

Satan's jealousy and his lust to *"… be like the Most High,"* were crushed when YHWH cast him out of heaven and instead created mankind in His likeness. Satan hates the human family profusely because mankind was created in the image of God, and when he sees mankind, he sees what he wanted for himself. When Satan sees man, he is inflamed with jealousy and provoked to destroy the image of God in man. It delights him to terrorize and disfigure the image of God in man through sickness and disease, hunger and violence. This explains why he takes pleasure in destroying the unborn before the image of God can be birthed into the world. Jesus said, *"You are of your father the devil, and the desires of your father you want to do. He was a murderer from the beginning..."* (John 8:44).

The battle for planet earth is an ancient and an ongoing war. When God planted Eden in the earth, it was a beachhead—a foothold from where He would restore His creation and impart His blessing into planet earth through His agent Adam and his offspring. *"...God, Who formed the earth and made it, Who has established it, Who did not create it in vain, Who formed it to be inhabited ..."* (Isaiah 45:18). If we examine Adam's commission in the original language, we see he was given authority to rule as king and to be the guardian and protector over the entire planet. An impartation of national sovereignty and jurisdiction was imparted to Adam. Through Adam and his offspring, God would produce a nation of sons to reestablish His blessings in all of the earth. Darkness covered the earth, and Adam's earthly activity as God's agent was to drive out the darkness and to reinstate God's blessing over all creation. This plan for mankind never got off the launching pad as Adam fell to the deceit of the Enemy before he could produce any offspring; however, the mission to bring healing to planet earth was reserved for another company of sons. *"...Go into all the world and preach the gospel to every creature"* (Mark 16:15). In his book, *Planet X*, Douglas Elwell asserts that mankind was meant to finish the job of subduing and controlling the earth: *"Thus, mankind was never meant to be independent of God, but instead exists solely for the purpose of subduing the dragon, of keeping it from ever rising again so that God should not have to defeat it again."*[22]

Let us examine the immense authority God bestowed upon Adam. Notice the words YHWH used when He enthroned Adam as the sovereign of the Earth: "*...let them have dominion* [over everything] ... *[28]Be fruitful and multiply; fill the earth and subdue it; have dominion over ... every living thing that moves ... [2:15]and God took the man and put him in the garden of Eden to tend and keep it*" (Genesis 1:26-28, 2:15, interpretation mine).

The words, *to tend and keep*, hold a military implication meaning "to guard and protect"—as one would guard a military outpost. The words *subdue it; have dominion over,* implies "taking control." Why would God commission Adam to guard and protect if there was not an adversary? Adam was anointed as a king, and YHWH crowned him with authority to rule the entire planet. He was clothed with the royal robe of the glory of God (Holy Spirit) to activate kingdom authority, "*fill the earth and subdue it.*"

Adam's ruling authority was demonstrated when he named all of the animals. "*...And whatever Adam called each living creature, that was its name*" (Genesis 2:19). For the casual reader, this statement seems insignificant; however, the student of the Word sees the power of the spoken word established through God's anointed agent. Adam's implementation of his role as king was confirmed as he set in motion the power of the spoken word. It is through the spoken word of God's anointed agents that His kingdom is established. "*For assuredly, I say to you, whoever says to this mountain, 'Be removed and be cast into the sea,' and does not doubt in his heart, but believes that those things he says will be done, he will have whatever he says*" (Mark 11:23).

---

[22]   Douglas A. Elwell, *PLANET X, The Sign of the Son of Man,* 88.

The power of the spoken word is demonstrated in the creation account. In Genesis 1:3, we are introduced to the "*Hayah*," a Hebrew action verb that is interpreted in English as, "Let there be." "*Then God said, 'Let there be [hayah] light'; and there was light.*" *Hayah* is the creative word of God, and its New Testament equivalent is the Greek word, *logos*. Through the spoken word of God (the *hayah*) Creation came into being. Through His spoken word, the visible appeared out of the invisible, and through the *hayah*, the spoken word of His agents, His will is accomplished.

CHAPTER 9

TRANSFERENCE OF AUTHORITY

"Then the Devil taking Him
Up on a very high mountain
Showed Him all the kingdoms of the
World in a moment of time. And
The Devil said unto Him, 'All this
authority I will give You, and their glory
For this has been delivered unto me, and
I give it to whomever I wish"
Luke 4:5

IF YOU CONSIDER THE enormity of the kingdom of darkness covering the world, you can grasp the extent of Adam's original authority. When Adam fell to the deception of Satan an occurrence of the transference of authority took place in the spiritual dimension that affected the whole course of human history. It was at this point in time that all governmental authority, the dominion and anointing that God had placed on His son Adam were legally transferred to Satan. When Satan declared, "...*All this authority ... has been delivered to me, and I give it to whomever I wish*" (Luke 4:6), he was rightfully validating his legal jurisdiction over Adam's former domain, to do with or to give to whomever he decided. In the last days Satan will find a man he has chosen to deliver his kingdom over to. The book of Revelation teaches us that all of the world will follow the serpent, and worship the dragon, (Revelation 13:2). This drastic change to the course of history and the shift in jurisdiction over planet earth Jesus called "*the Foundation of the World*" (John 17:24).

Throughout history many confrontations have occurred where "a transference of authority" have taken place. Like Adam we can take authority or we give authority away. For the believer to walk in victory a proper understanding of spiritual authority is vital. Understanding the dynamics of these incidents teaches the believer authentic spiritual authority and gives them confidence in who they are as sons of YHWH and how it affects their sovereignty. God has chosen the believer to be His agent to propagate the gospel and establish His authority in the earth so understanding the transference of authority enables the believer to identify spiritual opposition or YHWH's Kingdom authority.

The Greek word for *foundation* is *katabole,* meaning, "a deposition, a throwing down, the founding of an organization, company or entity." A legal deposition took place founding the "Kingdom of the World" under the rule and reign of Satan himself: *"All this authority I will give You, and their glory; for this has been delivered to me"* (Luke 4:6). When Adam fell under Satan's deception, and acceded to him, he legally transferred his dominion to Satan, and by the laws of heaven, the Kingdom of the World was founded. Isaiah 60:2 says,"...*behold the darkness shall cover the earth, and deep darkness the people...*" Once again God's plan to restore His blessing over creation was thwarted and set back for another time and for another man. The *"Foundation of the World"* has a direct bearing upon mankind's sovereignty placing them under the dominion of Satan, to truly regain sovereignty mankind has to be liberated from the power of the world and Satan it's ruler.

John 17:24-26, "... *You loved Me before <u>the foundation</u> <u>(katabole) of the world</u>. ²⁵O righteous Father! The world has not known You, but I have known You; and these have known that you sent Me. ²⁶And I have declared to them Your name...*"

Ephesians 1:4, 5, "*Just as He chose us in Him before <u>the foundation of the world</u>, that we should be holy and without blame before Him in love, ⁵having predestinated us to adoption as sons by Jesus Christ to Himself...*"

Hebrews 9:26, "*He then would have had to suffer often since <u>the foundation of the world</u>; but now, once at the end of the ages He has appeared to put away sin by the sacrifice of Himself.*"

1 Peter 1:20, "*He indeed was foreordained before <u>the foundation of the world</u>, but was manifest in these last times for you.*"

Revelation 13:8, "*All who dwell on the earth will worship him* [the Beast], *whose names have not been written in the Book of Life of the Lamb slain from <u>the foundation of the world</u>.*"

The first epic battle occurred in heaven when Lucifer tried to usurp YHWH's throne. "*And war broke out in heaven: Michael and his angels fought with the dragon; and the dragon and his angels fought, ⁸but they did not prevail, nor was a place found for them in heaven any longer*" (Revelation 12:7, 8). At this time Michael cast Satan and his angels out of heaven; "I saw Satan fall is lightning from heaven."

Traditional religious theology asserts that Satan has access to the throne of God where he continually appears to accuse the saints. Oh, how miserable and defeated these poor Christians must be to continually be under the power of Satan! They base their claim on Luke 22:31, Jesus said to Peter, "...*Simon, Simon! Indeed, Satan has asked for you, that he may sift you as wheat.*" They fail to take into account that at that time Jesus was still under the Old Covenant and pre-resurrection dispensation. They interpret Revelation 12 as taking place in the future Great Tribulation, with this interpretation they give the Accuser access to the throne of God until the last days. They glory in their misery and glorify sickness, poverty and afflictions making Job's confession, "*Though He slay me, yet will I trust Him*" (Job 13:15). That is a nice religious attitude to justify their lives of defeat but pulls other poor Christians down with them. These poor religious wretches never have the assurance of their victory over the Devil and do not possess the faith that Jesus has defeated the serpent and has occupied the alter of intercession where He continually prays for us. "*Seeing then that we have a great High Priest who has passed through the heavens, Jesus the Son of God ...*" (Hebrews 4:14). He is praying for you right now in a positive and redemptive way; He never accuses you and always excuses you. Satan has been defeated by the blood, the resurrection, and enthronement of Jesus. In the Old Testament, Satan continually accused the saints in the face of God, but today he no longer has access to God; instead, he accuses the saints to their own faces and Jesus has occupied the position of the great intercessor. Praise the LORD!

Satan is a legalist, and with everything he does he must circumvent, co-opt or undermine YHWH's universal laws. The entire universe operates within the confines of laws: the laws of gravity, magnetic laws, electrical laws, spiritual laws, etc. In order for anyone to operate within the laws of the universe, he must operate within the confines of law. Mankind is the possessor of and maintains jurisdiction over many invisible laws, including their free will. There are universal spiritual laws that Satan has learned to circumvent.

He understands the Law of the Transference of Authority and is the master usurper of power and the "underminer" of all legal authority. He has perfected the art of deception in order to co-opt and subvert the free will of mankind. Deception is used to capture the consent of mankind and to incite humanity to war against the Creator. This is where the ancient art of magic or deception originated.

The law of "free will" prohibits Satan from encroaching upon on an individual unless he obtains consent. Through deception, mankind grants Satan consent by relinquishing his sovereign rights. The breakdown of free will occurs during times of weakness or trauma and creates an opening for Satan to do things that would otherwise normally be blocked. The art of magic is the art of deception. The art Satan has perfected to take advantage of mankind. He has learned how to break down the free will of mankind through trauma, fear, confusion and sin. He would have no power to abort and kill the unborn if he were not given consent by humanity. Governments would not have the power of war if they did not obtain the consent of the people.

When Satan took Jesus to the mount of temptation his objective was to trick Jesus' into giving him the Kingdom of God through deception. Satan assumed that Jesus was weak since He had not eaten in forty days and chose to attack Him in his weakness.

> "...the devil, taking Him up on a high mountain, showed Him all the kingdoms of the world in a moment of time. [6]And the devil said to Him, "All this authority I will give You, and their glory, for this has been delivered to me, and I give it to whomever I wish. [7]Therefore, if You will worship before me, all will be Yours."
>
> And Jesus answered and said to him, "Get behind Me, Satan! For it is written, 'You shall worship YHWH your God, and Him only you shall serve.'" (Luke 4:4-8).

His encounter established His victory over Satan and reversed Adam's failure. Satan's first temptation was to undermine His standing as God's Son, testing His identity, "...*If you are the Son of God...*" (Luke 4:3). Satan had already tricked God's first son into delivering his authority over to him, and for the second time he was making a play for all of God's created order. He knew this was the home-run, the grand-slam play that would bring down YHWH God's entire order and deliver it over to him. What he didn't know was that Jesus did not come to reclaim Adam's authority He came to establish His own authority.

When Satan showed Jesus all the kingdoms of the world in a moment of time Jesus' perception was not of geographic states and nations but His perception was in the spiritual dimension (the third eye). His observation was of the spiritual kingdom of Babylon manifested on earth with and all demonic networks in the world; the networks of terrorism, the networks of religion and idolatry, the networks of greed and riches, the kingdoms of tyranny and injustice, drugs and addictions, the epidemics of sickness and disease, death and destruction, and the illegitimate governments of this world. All of this authority Satan had corrupted and reprogrammed to destroy the human race and to war against YHWH the God of creation

The Devil's scheme was to trick the Son of God into bowing down and worshipping him. Just one little act of iniquity from Jesus and he would triumph over YHWH and topple His dominion. It seemed simple—just one little act of worshipping the Devil, and all would be His. "...*if You will worship before me, all will be Yours*" (Luke 4:7). He knew that if Jesus, a man under the law, broke the First Commandment, all the curses of the law would come into force. The Devil knew the consequences of breaking the First Commandment' remember the command of God: "*I am the Lord* [YHWH] *your God ... ⁷You shall have no other gods before Me ... ⁹you shall <u>not</u>*

bow down to them nor serve them. For I, the Lord [YHWH] *your God, am a jealous God, visiting the iniquity of the fathers upon the children..."* (Deuteronomy 5:6, 7, 9).

Jesus came as a man under the Law and was commissioned to fulfill all of the Law every jot and tittle. Satan was stupid to think Jesus would be tempted to desire all that was in the world and their glory and he misjudged the piety of Jesus. It seemed simple enough; just one act of bowing before the Devil and He would regain all Adam had lost. Unfortunately for the Devil, his play to usurp the kingdom of YHWH God from the Son of God was his vein imagination The nature of the kingdom of Satan is chaos, and its final destination cannot stand. What Satan didn't know was that Jesus *didn't* want authority in the world; He came in His own authority to establish His own kingdom. He had authority over the world. "*...All authority has been given to Me in heaven and on earth*" (Matthew 28:18). Notice the scripture does not say "in the world", but says, *"all authority in heaven and on earth"*—not in the world which belongs to **Satan**.

The DNA of mankind and his core nature is wired to worship God and to be united and in harmony with the heavenly *Agapeo.*"*God is Spirit, and those who worship Him must worship in spirit and truth*" (John 4:24). Since Jesus came in the form of man, the Devil was counting on the *"Mystery of Iniquity"* to appear and corrupt the Son of Man. The *"Mystery of Iniquity"* is the appearance of the adulterous nature and the perversion of the spirit of worship. The Devil perfected the art of defiling YHWH's dwelling place in the heart of man when Adam bowed to him and with the corruption of the rest of humanity. The *"Mystery of Iniquity"* spoken by the apostle Paul in 2 Thessalonians 2:7 is man's innate nature that is adulterous and betrays his Creator.

> You shall have no other gods before Me. *You shall not make for yourself a carved image—any likeness of anything that is in heaven above, or that is in the earth beneath, or that is in the water under the earth; *you shall not bow down to

them nor serve them. For I, the Lord [YHWH] *your God,*
am a jealous God ... (Exodus 20:3-5).

YHWH's heart desire for His intelligent created being is for an exclusive love relationship with Him. Worship is the highest form of expressing one's love for the Creator. All humanity is wired to worship God; if it is not God, man will worship something else. Man can never be complete until he becomes one with his Creator through worship. When God created mankind, He placed within his core nature an innate desire to connect with Him through love and worship. Unfortunately, with the freedom of choice, comes the right to worship something of one's own choosing.

When man's worshipping nature is perverted and turned toward something other than YHWH, it becomes *idolatry*, which is "the act of worshipping false gods," whereas *iniquity* is, "the adulterous nature that provokes one to idolatry"; *iniquity* and *idolatry* are synonymous throughout scripture. "*For rebellion is as the sin of witchcraft, and stubbornness is as iniquity and idolatry* ..." (1 Samuel 15:23).

There would be no betrayal by Jesus; His declaration established His exclusive standing with the heavenly Father and announced His new jurisdiction. At the temptation, Jesus rebuked the Devil. "... *Get behind Me, Satan! For it is written,* '*You shall worship the Lord* [YHWH] *your God, and Him only you shall serve*" (Luke 4:8). "*I was also blameless before Him, and I kept myself from my iniquity*" (Psalm 18:23). When Jesus turned His back on Satan, He deprived the Devil of conquest putting him in his place! He thwarted iniquity. He crushed the Enemy's attempt to seize the throne of YHWH. A better interpretation of this verse in the original Greek would be, "*Get out of My face, Satan!*" This version is more accurate because it is the face-to-face relationship that God desires with mankind, and worship is a face-to-face encounter with God.

Satan has always desired to have a face-to-face station with God. The Protestant reformers referred to the face-to-face relationship with God as *coram Deo*— *"All life is lived before the face of God."*[23]

From our narrative, we learned that in antiquity Satan had access to the face of YHWH. Even after he fell from his place in heaven, he continued to present himself with the sons of God. In Job chapter one, he is with the sons of God, and in the book of Zechariah he is standing in the presence of God next to the High Priest. From that location, Satan accused the saints and repeatedly attacked God's people down through the ages. *"And the Lord said, 'Simon, Simon! Indeed, Satan has asked for you."* (Luke 22:31)

The power of the blood of Jesus and His resurrection is profound. Jesus not only made atonement for all the sins of mankind but He also cleansed heaven of the defilement that Satan brought there. After the resurrection, Jesus ascended to the throne of God with His precious blood, sprinkled it on the mercy seat, and made atonement in the heavenlies. He grabbed Satan by the hair and cast him out of heaven once and for all! *"But God will wound the head of His enemies, the hairy scalp of the one who still goes on in his trespasses"* (Psalm 68:21). Through the cross and the resurrection, Jesus took His place in heaven as our High Priest and cast the Devil out. Now, no devil or demon can ever come between Him and the Father to accuse the saints. *"So, the great dragon was cast out, that old serpent, called the Devil and Satan, who deceives the whole world; he was cast to the earth, and his angels were cast out with him"* (Revelation 12:9).

What the Devil hadn't counted on was that Jesus did not come to reclaim Adam's authority. Jesus did not want power in the world; He had power *over* the world. He came in His

---

23   R. C. Sproul, "What Does coram Deo Mean?" Ligonier Ministries, 27 May 2015, www.ligonier.org/blog/ (*Ligonier.org>what-does-coream- deo-mean/*), accessed 18 June 2016.

own authority to establish a new dominion. He did not come to regain the power of the world but to destroy the works of the Devil. Adam's authority was inconsequential; His authority is greater. He did not say, "All power in the world has been given to me." He said, "...*All authority has been given to Me in heaven and on earth*" (Matthew 28:18). When Jesus said, "*But if I cast out demons by the Spirit of God, surely the kingdom of God has come upon you,*" (Matthew 12:28), He was announcing His authority over the power of Satan's dominion. In other words, there was a new sheriff in town. Jesus came to destroy the works of the Devil, and once and for all put down his reign of terror.

When Jesus was anointed with the Holy Spirit at His water baptism a new impartation of national sovereignty and jurisdiction was given to Him, a new dispensation to establish the Kingdom of YHWH and His heavenly family. The same mission God had given to Adam and his descendants, the same mission given to Abraham, and the same mission given to Israel. Jesus articulated the mission plan in Matthew 6:9, "*Our Father in heaven, hallowed be Your name. Your kingdom come. Your will be done. On earth as it is in heaven.*" He came proclaiming the kingdom of YHWH, a new rule, a new dominion, a new culture, a new King, and God's jurisdiction on earth. "...*The time is fulfilled, and the kingdom of God is at hand. Repent, and believe in the gospel*" (Mark 1:15).

CHAPTER 10

A NEW REFORMATION

"Now it shall come to pass in the later days
That the mountain of the Lord's [YHWH's] house
Shall be established on the top of the mountains,
And shall be exalted above the hills;
And all nations shall flow to it."
(Isaiah 2:2)

THE REFORMATION WE ARE about to see is the mass rejection of a failed institutional church model and the transformation of believers into the family of YHWH God. We are seeing mass corruption being exposed on every level in the world today. Christianity will experience a similar upheaval with a separation between an entrenched religious system and the righteous on an unparalleled level. Unfortunately, the church will fall under the judgment of God the same way Israel fell under His judgment; however true believers will be separated from the Babylonian religious system and will be preserved from the wrath of God.

In the 1960s we were given a glimpse of an organic move of God. The hippie movement and the fledgling charismatic movement ushered in small group, home movements and communal living. Unfortunately, the movement was pressured back into the failed model of church, and most charismatics settled back into the comforts of organized church. This next move will open seekers' eyes to the illusion of church because a new vision of the family of God will be clearly revealed and a better way into sonship will be shown.

Throughout history, every new move of God has been persecuted by the old move. We will see persecution of true believers by the established religious system on an unparalleled level. True seekers are ostracized and sidelined by mainline churches, "*They will put you out of the synagogues; yes, the time is coming that whoever kills you will think that he offers God service. ³And these things they will do because they have not known the Father nor Me*" (John 16:2, 3).

I use the term "seekers" in reference to hungry souls who never stop in their pursuit of God. *Seekers* is a politically correct term commonly used by Churches when referring to the unsaved; however, we should never cease being seekers. In the sermon on the mount, Jesus said, "*Blessed are those who hunger and thirst for righteousness, for they shall be filled*" (Matthew 5:6). It is my hunger for more of God that continually drives me to seek Him.

Jesus' victory over Satan in the wilderness temptation paved the way for the body of Christ to be birthed and to be clothed with kingdom authority. On the day of Pentecost, the body of Christ was empowered with the Holy Spirit, and they effectively spread the gospel into the known world. There were no borders to the gospel, and believers preached freely and without fear. With the empowerment of the Holy Spirit, the mission of the early ecclesia was so successful that by the fourth century Christianity's success became their worst enemy, when they became the official state religion of the Roman Empire. Unfortunately, the success of the move of God became its worst enemy, and a transference of authority away from the church began sapping inherent spiritual authority away from God's people.

Christianity took a turn to western thought through the influence of Greek writers and early Christian apologists in the second and third centuries and by the turn of the fourth century, Roman Emperor Constantine paved the way for Christianity to be declared the official state religion. Constantine convened the Nicene Council where church leaders canonized religious thought and church structure around a Babylonian model, further solidifying the institutionalization of the church. This turn, neutered Christianity of its inherent power, removing it from the theocratic rule of God and placing it under the authority structure of man.

Deception comes in many forms and has become deeply embedded in the fabric of the church. Today, we are living in a world where the church has been effectively neutralized, and the spirit of Babylon has subtly taken control. The institutionalization of the church effectively neutralized the inherent authority of the sovereign "family of YHWH." The institutionalizing of the church created a counterfeit—a very close image of the real thing, but nevertheless a counterfeit. The conspiracy to neutralize the church has been a long-term scheme, and the Enemy crept under the radar of the protectors of the church. So-called modern apostles and prophets, who have no real vision from God and have been co-opted by the spirit of Babylon perpetuating an institutional model called church. Jesus warned the disciples to beware of the leaven of the Sadducees and Pharisees.

Western Christianity, or the "*church*," was canonized under Constantine. The word church is not a biblical word but was derived from the Greek word *circa*, circle, or circus. No one really knows where the word church comes from but Biblical interpreters replaced the word ecclesia, "the called-out ones", with the word church. The western concept of church imprisoned the minds of ministers and church was normalized. Christian congregations adopted the form of church around religious concepts that have kept them bound for centuries. Although Luther's Reformation in the 1500s revived the doctrine of salvation through faith alone, it perpetuated the tradition of the western church model. Church fathers began to herd the flock of God, guiding them away from the more organic *oikos model of the household of God* toward a more authoritarian and organized model.

Today's modern church continues to build institutional models missing the more organic concept of *"the family of YHWH."* Christian missionaries' go into all of the world and build churches, whereas Jesus' concept is to go into all the world and make sovereign sons. So-called modern apostles and prophets take pride and boast in the fact that they have planted churches and orphanages around the world; unfortunately, they have planted institutions. So-called apostles and prophets have evolved into authoritarians or into a touchy-feely grace-based doctrines catering to emotional needs yet leaving their followers locked up in the Babylonian system. These so-called apostles and prophets have no vision from God; if they did, we would see their fruit in a revolutionary message to free God's people from the spiritual DNA of Babylon.

Western civilization has given the world institutions to satisfy all of the needs and insecurity of all the people. We have institutions for education, healthcare, finance, insane asylums, prisons, warfare, law and order, human services, disaster protection, religion, government, the United Nations and so forth. In the western mindset, institutions are the highest form of civilization that organizes and satisfies all of the needs of the poor and huddled masses. And of course, to house these institutions, we have churches, cathedrals, skyscrapers, cities, and monuments of a ziggurat-building society. God's people and the church are locked up in that system! Israel became locked up in Jeroboam's religious system and from the beginning of his reign until Israel was scattered into all the world they never repented. The church has become so lost in the Babylonian religious system they can't repent and will go into judgment because of that.

In all of our manmade systems we lose the value of YHWH God's heavenly vision—the model of "the *heavenly family.*" Of this one thing I am sure: the institutionalized church is incapable of producing the sovereign sons of YHWH. Institutions can produce Christians and religious people, but only fathers can produce sons; only families can rear and nurture sons. Church institutions have no seed in themselves; only fathers carry the seed. Our heavenly Father created mankind with life-producing seed in fathers, and He created the model of the family (*oikos*) to birth and nurture children.

If you were to envision the heavenly family model of the ecclesia, what do you think that would look like? The enemy's plan has been to blind God's people from seeing what has been right before their eyes. Jesus warned us not to be blinded by the leaven of the Sadducees and Pharisees. The Sin of Jeroboam in 1 Kings 12:25-34 was to divert his people away from worshipping God according to YHWH's divine order. God's command was for Israel to keep His feasts in Jerusalem; however, Jeroboam set up idols in Bethel and Dan to prevent God's people from going to Jerusalem. He commanded his people to worship in the new places of his making, Constantine did the same thing in creating the "church". Like Jeroboam he installed a false priesthood to serve in the temples and high places and Israel never repented of this sin for hundreds of years leading to their banishment from the land. I believe the first six seals in Revelation will be God's judgment on the church to separate the righteous from the religious.

Today, the family unit is persistently under the Enemy's attack trying to corrupt YHWH's divine order. On Indian reservations, the father figure has been effectively removed from the households, leaving generations of young men never being fathered and the move of God has been supplanted by the church. On our Indian reservations we have grown men who are still boys, the institutions of tribal councils were established and a socialistic approach to civilize the Indians. Unfortunately, the more social engineering they attempted on the Natives through government institutions, programs and religion, the more they destroyed traditional family units. Culturally, Native Americans never had institutions; rather, they had fathers and families and kinship units i.e., tribes. *"Honor your father and your mother, as the Lord [YHWH] your God has commanded you, that your days may be long, and that it may be well with you in the land which the Lord [YHWH] your God is giving you"* (Deuteronomy 5:16).

The neutralizing of the church effectively removed it from its ruling authority and rendered it useless in spiritual warfare. The promises of Jesus to an overcoming church in Revelation chapters two and three quickly invoked the curses pronounced upon their failure. History shows how the seven churches of Revelation all succumbed to the rise of Islam. In one hundred years, Islam invaded and conquered all of the progress Christianity had made in its first three hundred years. By 690 A.D. Islam was building an abomination on the temple mount in Jerusalem known as the Dome on the Rock, proclaiming, *"There is no god but Allah, Muhammad is his prophet, and he has no children."* A spiritually weak, anemic institutionalized church was unable to effectively combat the powers of darkness and left the skeleton and dry bones and cathedrals scattered across the globe. The failure of the church gave rise to the greatest threat of all, Islam, and the spirit of Antichrist. As I have said, *"What you fail to confront on the spiritual level, you will eventually have to confront in the natural."*

The first thing Christians do when they establish a church is surrender their sovereignty. In the spirit of accountability, they relinquish their sovereignty by going under the headship of the man/church/government/ religious complex, aka, Babylon. Becoming an institution locks up the rule of God outside the institution and puts it under the rule of man, i.e., Satan. By incorporating and registering as 501(c)(3) and 501(c)(4) IRS tax-exempt status, churches surrender their sovereignty and bow to another god—the government. The First Commandment says, "*You shall have no other gods above me*" (Exodus 20:2, my interpretation). The United States was a cleverly designed constitution for the separation of church and state; however, the Enemy undermined the constitution with the introduction of the IRS and social programs to bring the church under the authority of the government in spite of the fact that early Americans were here for religious freedom. When Christians incorporate, they are changing their identity from sonship to citizenship. They change their address from seated in heavenly places to seated on the board of directors. Today's mega churches, denominations, and even small independent churches are perpetuating the failed model of an incorporated institutional church. No wonder miracles and healings have ceased in American churches. It is insane for the church to continue to perpetuate a failed model. We have removed Him from the throne of our hearts and have given ourselves to false gods.

In a survey of the most respected professions, the profession of "pastor" is near the bottom—just above "car salesman."

- 4,000 new churches begin each year, and 7,000 churches close.

- Over 1,700 pastors left the ministry every month last year.

- Over 1,300 pastors were terminated by the local church each month, many without cause.

- Over 3,500 people a day left the church last year.[24]

---

[24] "Statistics in the Ministry," *Pastoral Care, Inc.*, 2016, http://www. pastoralcareinc.com/statistics, accessed 18 June 2016.

We are entering a new age of reformation where more and more Christians are leaving the church, realizing it does not work and that there is a need for fresh revelation of the divine order. The first order of business is to re-establish their divine sovereignty. As I mentioned earlier, this requires a change of mind and perspective. Christians need to break free and take control of their own destiny! Salvation is about our intimate, face-to-face relationship with YHWH and protecting our standing as His sovereign sons. What believers need to understand is when they are redeemed through the blood of Jesus, they are not only delivered from sin but are restored to their original standing as sons of God with their birthright fully restored. The sons of YHWH must break free from manmade systems and institutions.

My own journey led me through the maze of religion and institutionalized worship. As a young evangelist, I was always taught that I needed to be in submission to leadership. Humility was emphasized and to minister outside of some kind of covering was viewed as being rebellious or prideful. The pressure of the institution was always there to keep me in submission, which I thought was the honorable thing to do. I was fortunate to find a worldwide organization that was compatible with my doctrinal beliefs and my apostolic father, Don Kridor, was a model of love and authority. His was a wonderful ministry, but the distance between churches and headquarters kept individual pastors isolated and lacking fellowship. Please don't misunderstand me; I believe in submission but to YHWH's proper authorities and not to man.

Through a series of visions and circumstances Holy Spirit led me to pioneer a church on the Flathead Indian Reservation. In the beginning, the church operated as an independent entity with my ministry covering from my pastor and home church, River of Life Fellowship, in Bozeman, Montana. In the beginning, we saw hundreds of salvations as we went from house to house, jails, and church services in a motel. People were hungry and excited about our ministry, and church attendance grew rapidly. While we were experiencing revival our home church in Bozeman folded. The leadership scattered, leaving us praying about a church covering.

Our desperation to be under a church covering exposed us to several different types of church structures, with a little bit of pressure to join. We met apostolic ministries, organizations that advocated rulership by elders, rule by pastors, sole corporations and we eventually joined a major Pentecostal denomination that held doctrinal beliefs that were similar to ours. Our new denomination, the International Church of the Foursquare Gospel, believe in a "modified Episcopal system," which basically is rule by bishops. These semi-independent churches are operated by a church council with the pastor supposedly as the head but answerable to the bishop. It seemed at the time that our church gained some credibility and respect in the community.

While the church was becoming respectable in the community, I could sense that we were losing respect from the Holy Spirit. The pressure to bring the church into proper institutional order and to have a functioning church council resulted in the selection of individuals who were not spiritually mature. Church council meetings took on an adversarial spirit, and, as a result, church attendance dropped off. It seemed that the people with goodly spirits began to drop out, and a cliché of relatives began to take control of the church. A dispute over electing an individual to the church council resulted in calling our church overseer to mediate the dispute. From that point, everything seemed to go in the wrong direction.

I sought counsel from fellow pastors, rebuked the spirit of Jezebel and cried out to God. I earnestly prayed, sought God for the answers, and finally the Holy Spirit spoke to me, *"There is an institutionalized spirit of Jezebel in all denominations."* I was stunned but I shook the dust off of my feet and walked away from my beloved church. Finally, my eyes began to be opened to the fallacy of what I had been trying to perpetuate. At first, like most of my brother pastors, I clung to the church model, praying that she could be reformed. It has taken a while, but my search finally led me to the conclusions presented in this book.

What is needed is a revolution of ideas, a new paradigm, and a fresh perspective. The church has been locked up in this religious cycle for so long that the Spirit of YHWH has been unable to penetrate There is a battle for your mind, and you believe only what you accept is true and have emotionally adopted. If you have been locked into the failed church model, you can only believe what you know and have been taught. Our eyes must be open to the illusion for change to come and one must to be willing to repent and change his mindset.

Having ministered on Indian reservations for over forty years, I have been concerned about the abundant amount of backsliding among born-again Christians. Pastors and churches are isolated and experience poverty, persecution and spiritual oppression. Most have fasted and prayed and earnestly sought God to find a remedy for the lukewarmness in the church, and they usually conclude that more prayer and fasting are needed to usher in the next great revival. We must come to our senses and realize that the reason for endless backsliding is because we are trying to plug new believers into a failed model. This cycle continues until even the dogs are worn out. I call this insanity! Trying the same thing in the same way over and over again and expecting different results is insanity. A new paradigm shift goes for indigenous churches around the world. Instead of welcoming new believers into the family of God, we indoctrinate them into church protocol. The first thing we do when we get one saved is turn them into good white men and faithful church people. When I was a young Christian, I cannot tell you the amount of time my pastors spent telling us to be faithful to the church no matter how hard it gets. We were quickly indoctrinated into church culture. We were told that there are three things we must do: read our Bibles, pray, and find a church to attend. We weren't told about becoming the family of YHWH because preachers only knew the church model. However, in spite of all this the reason YHWH is going to begin His move on the reservations is because most independent Native churches are not under the man-made government church model and they are not far off of the Oikos model of the heavenly family.

Isn't there something odd about a native pastor on a reservation, standing behind the pulpit in a three-piece suit? That was me! You would have thought I was on Wall Street. I can't tell you the number of pictures on church missionary boards I have seen of African ministers wearing a three-piece suit with his Bible in hand. Yet this is the model we were given. Where did we get the idea that the highest form of holiness and glorifying YHWH was to become a good white man wearing a three-piece suit? I don't think Jesus wears a three-piece suit. As young Christians we were taught that anything Native was of the Devil. We were discouraged from attending powwows or cultural gatherings for fear we might backslide. One of the men in my fellowship told me a story of an encounter he had with an Assembly of God pastor when he was a young Christian. This brother had just gotten saved and was on fire for God. He decided to wear his best clothes to church, which was a traditional native ribbon shirt.

> When he entered the church, the pastor stopped him and exclaimed, *"I'm sorry, but we don't allow these types of shirts in this church. By the way, what do all of those ribbons represent? Offerings to demons or what?"*

The young brother looked at the pastor and said, *"What is that silk tie you are wearing around your neck? Is that some type of offering to demons?"*

A very dangerous trend is taking place in the modern church that is ushering in an unholy alliance between church the state and the spirit of Islam. On the horizon looms a melding of the church, the government and the spirit of Islam that the sons of YHWH will confront now and in the near future. I am afraid to say that many will lose their heads. We are seeing religious institutions coming under the banner of unity and tolerance, with leaders proclaiming, "We all worship the same God—even if he is called by different names. According to Pope Francis in his latest teaching, *"We all serve the same God."* Even Protestant pastors such as Rick Warren and other liberal pastors have endorsed a hybrid religion, they call *Chrislam*, which is an amalgamation of Christianity and Islam. The handwriting is on the wall! This dangerous trend should be called out for what it is—the spirit of Antichrist.

Islam is the most Antichrist quasi religion/government entity that has ever existed. Allah is the antithesis of YHWH, and there can never be a compromise. To become a Muslim, a person must renounce all other gods, including the God of all creation (YHWH); and he must deny that Jesus is the Son of God. To become Muslim, a person must deny the existence of the holy Trinity and confess that "Allah is god, there is no other, and he does not have any children." *"Who is a liar but he who denies that Jesus is the Christ? He is antichrist who denies the Father and the Son"* (1 John 2:22).

We are living in the day where the cry has gone out of heaven: *"...Come out of her, my people, lest you share in her sins, and lest you receive not of her plagues. ⁵For her sins have reached to heaven, and God has remembered her iniquities"* (Revelation 18:4, 5). Those who choose to cling to their religion and government will be held accountable for her sins and will pay the penalty for standing with her. YHWH is interested in a family of sovereign sons who are not subject to any man or system but are full-grown mighty men of valor who can root out the powers of darkness and establish the dominion of the kingdom of God. *"The LORD {YHWH} shall send the rod of Your strength out of Zion. Rule in the midst of Your enemies!"* (Psalm 110:2).

The transformation of the church in these last days will be from nominal Christians into the sovereign sons of *YHWH*. The first three hundred years of the early church was a time of rapid increase. *"Therefore, those who were scattered went everywhere preaching the word"* (Acts 8:4). Believers lived under the direct guidance of YHWH through the Holy Spirit. They were not confined by borders nor were they under the jurisdiction of kings or governments, but they boldly proclaimed the kingdom of God. Miracles and healings were a normal part of early Christian experience.

An infantile movement of Christians is turning away from the church and awakening to a new move of God. A fresh prophetic word is announcing a new move, and believers must be ready for something new. Most are expecting something new but are asking, *"What does it look like?"* And others are expecting the church to reform itself. Jesus prophesied to the disciples in Matthew 24:2, *"... Assuredly, I say to you, not one stone shall be left here upon another, that shall not be thrown down."* This is the fate of institutional Christianity! The religious institution that has held God's people captive must come down.

The Holy Spirit's message for the church; it will suffer the same fate as Israel because they practice the "Sin of Jeroboam". The sin of Jeroboam had two basic tenants, establishing false places of worship (idolatry), and ordaining a false priesthood. Jeroboam feared that if the children of Israel continued to go to Jerusalem on the feast days that their hearts would be turned away from him. So, he set up false idols in Bethel and Dan and established his own feast days commanding Israel to worship God there. They built worship places on the mountains and high hills and disobeyed God's commandments and feast days. The Bible says that Israel never repented of the sin of Jeroboam and this resulted in God's wrath falling on them. The church fell into the sin of Jeroboam during the reign of Constantine. The carefully crafted church model that emerged from Nicene council was designed to gather God's people in a worship setting that would satisfy their religious craving yet prevent them from tapping into the dimension of Holy Spirit and His divine governmental order. In addition, a false order of priesthood was ordained to preside over the alters of deception. As we see the family of God emerge, we will see a new kind of child of God that does not resemble Christians and the church people of the past. The era of going to church on Sunday and then back to the comforts of the world for the rest of the week will be reformed into Holy Spirit filled believers walking in faith and the power of the Spirit 24/7. The sons of God will experience supernatural phenomena of the kingdom of God on a daily basis. Please understand that when I say the "sons of God," I am referring to all believers whether they are male or female, and when I refer to "fathers," I am referring to those in the body of Christ who are spiritual fathers and mothers, and the Apostle Paul spoke of the spiritual sons of God.

> *"For you are all sons of God through faith in Christ Jesus. [27] For as many of you as were baptized into Christ have put on Christ. [28] There is neither Jew nor Greek, there is neither slave nor free, there is neither male nor female; for you are all one in Christ Jesus"* (Galatians 3:26-28).

The sons of God will be marked by their anointing to teach all nations, *ethnos* groups, to baptize believers, and bring healing to the land (Romans 8:19).They will walk in the Great Commission commanded by Jesus in Matthew 28:19, "*Go therefore and make disciples of all the nations, baptizing them in the name of the Father and of the Son and of the Holy Spirit.*"The government of God will return to the family nations model that YHWH ordained from the beginning. We will see His Nations emerge in the earth and His kingdom established. Is it a fearful thing to be under the government of God? YHWH's calendar will be reinstituted and Sun dials used in place of the fake Babylonian moon calendar of the Jews and the Gregorian Greek mythology calendar. YHWH's people will celebrate His feast days and sabbaths on the correct dates and not on the dates of the Roman empire. Instead of having celebrities and stars as our pastors we will have fathers and mothers loving and nurturing their families as their own children and feeding them the food of heaven which is the word of God.

The family of YHWH will be marked by their adherence to a new model of water baptism. Jesus commanded His apostles to go into all the world and baptize them in the name of the Father, and of the Son, and of the Holy Spirit. That means exactly what it says! In their names! This is another spot where the leaven of the Sadducees and Pharisees subverted the word of God and changed it to divert believers away from the names of YHWH. Water baptism is an act of entering into a covenant with YHWH and changing our identity from our old man into a new identity as YHWH's children. God's sons will be baptized in the name of the Father, YHWH, in the name of the Son, Yahshua, and in the name of the Holy Spirit, EliYah.

CHAPTER 11

THE MINISTRY OF JESUS CHRIST

"Behold what manner of love the Father has bestowed on us, that we should be called the sons of God…"
(1 John 3:1)

WE ARE ON THE threshold of the greatest move of God the world has ever seen. We will be on the cutting edge or we will be left in our own strength, trying to perpetuate a failed model. When we examine the church in the world today, the logical conclusion is a weak, anemic conglomeration of Christians barely holding on, trying to save the whole world by creating models of their own futility. In spite of this, there is a dramatic growth in the house church movement around the world where there is minimal interference from the institutional church. The church, or more correctly the *oikos*— "the family of YHWH"—is in desperate need of spiritual edification and a higher level of anointing from the ministry. I challenge the *oikos* to increase the level of anointing in their personal lives so as to raise the level of edification in the body of Christ. The challenge for the body of Christ today is to become the *oikos*—the family of YHWH where Jesus is free to manifest His ministry.

It is time for a change; a new wave is coming!

There is a ministry in the world today where miracles follow wherever He goes. When He goes to Africa, multitudes are saved, healed and delivered. When He goes to Asia, mighty manifestations of the power of God accompany His preaching. Wherever He preaches in the world, revival breaks out and multitudes are saved and healed. The gospels give us a glimpse at the greatest Minister who ever lived. He is the greatest example after whom we have to pattern our ministries. *"Jesus Christ is the same yesterday, today, and forever"* (Hebrews 13:8). Jesus was a man who manifested the glory and power of YHWH. He came preaching the kingdom of God in the demonstration of the power of the Holy Spirit. Our challenge is to move out of religious manmade ministries and into the greater works ministry that Jesus promised in John 14:12 *"... the works that I do he will do also; and greater works than these he will do, because I go to My Father."*

The model YHWH gave His sons to pattern after came in the form of a man—Jesus, the Archetype. He is our prime example of a man being enabled by God to do the works of the Father. Jesus was clothed with the mantle of the Holy Spirit to activate kingdom authority. YHWH set His seal of approval upon Him.

> *When He had been baptized, Jesus came up immediately from the water; and behold, the heavens were opened to Him, and He saw the Spirit of God descending like a dove and alighting upon Him. [17]And suddenly a voice came from heaven, saying, "This is My beloved Son, in whom I am well pleased"* (Matthew 3:16, 17).

The confirmation that Jesus was indeed perfect was twofold: first, When the Spirit descended and remained upon Him at His baptism, and secondly, His resurrection. Jesus could not have been raised from the dead if sin had been found in Him. The ministry and the message that He preached were confirmed with signs and wonders. Prior to His baptism, Jesus never operated in His ministry. At His baptism in the river Jordan, the Holy Spirit descended in the form of a dove, lit upon Jesus and YHWH spoke out of heaven: *"... You are My beloved Son, in whom I am well pleased"* (Mark 1:11). John the Baptist gave witness and said, *"...Upon whom you see the Spirit descending, and remaining on Him, this is He who baptizes with the Holy Spirit"* (John 1:33). This was the full manifestation of the Godhead in a human body. The perfect uniting of God and man to accomplish the works of the Father on earth. *"That is, that God was in Christ reconciling the world unto himself." (2 Corinthians 5:19)*

God never intended to dwell in temples made by the hands of man, as the prophet said, *"Heaven is My throne, and earth is My footstool. Where is the house that will you build Me? And where is the place of My rest? Says the Lord [YHWH]"* (Isaiah 66:1, 2). YHWH has always desired to dwell within human vessels. God created mankind to be the dwelling place of the Holy Spirit, but because of mankind's fallen condition, the Spirit could not dwell in sinful flesh. *"And the Lord said, 'My Spirit shall not strive with man forever, for he is indeed flesh ...'"* (Genesis 6:3). He has been seeking a habitation for a long time and found it in the perfect sinless vessel of His Son. Jesus was the perfect vessel prepared from begore the foundation of the earth for the indwelling of the Holy Spirit.

Jesus was not only filled with the Spirit, but He was also baptized in the Holy Spirit; the Holy Spirit was inside and outside. *"Then Jesus, being filled with the Holy Spirit, returned from the Jordan and was led by the Spirit..."* (Luke 4:1). Jesus announced, *"The Spirit of the Lord [YHWH] is upon me, because He has anointed Me to preach the gospel ..."* (Luke 4:18). These verses point out that the sons of YHWH must be filled with the Holy Spirit and be baptized in the Holy Spirit. Many doctrines confuse the issue by purporting that the baptism of the

Holy Spirit is the indwelling spirit, while others stress the outward baptism or speaking in tongues. However, in order to fulfill the Father's will, it is necessary for the Holy Spirit to be in us and upon us. Jesus made this possible by becoming the *new wine skin* within the child of God for the Holy Spirit to fill. *"But you are not in the flesh but in the Spirit, if indeed the Spirit of God dwells in you. Now if anyone does not have the Spirit of Christ, he is not His"* (Romans 8:9).

Just like Jesus was baptized with the Holy Spirit, we must also be baptized with the Holy Spirit, which includes speaking in tongues. I was confused for many years about the difference between the Spirit of Christ and the Holy Spirit. I finally realized that we are baptized into the Spirit of Christ by the Holy Spirit at the new birth (1 Corinthians 12:13), and then we are baptized into the Holy Spirit by Jesus (Luke 3:16). These are two different experiences. We must be born of the Spirit of Christ in order for the mantle of the Holy Spirit to empower us. Just like Adam, we must wear the mantle of the glory of God to be fully clothed. The baptism of the Holy Spirit, activates Kingdom authority. The restoration of speaking in tongues is as vital as the rest of our spiritual senses. Obedience to the Holy Spirit includes praying in our prayer language, which releases the fountains of living water within the believer. The reason the disciples were not confused about speaking in tongues on the day of Pentecost is because Jesus was an example to them in His prayer life.

It was necessary for Jesus to remain in submission to the Holy Spirit in order to lay the legal framework for mankind to operate in His ministry. To legally establish His kingdom, He could not operate in His capacity as God while in His physical body. Everything He did was through the Holy Spirit and by the operation of faith. As God, He had the authority to command legions of angels or to call down brimstone on His enemies, yet He chose to walk in submission to the Spirit— even if it killed Him. Jesus laid the ground rules for the body of Christ to operate through His ministry. Believers operate under the same principles and legal requirements as Jesus did. The same things Jesus did, we can do also and greater works than these because Jesus seized the headship and sits at the right hand of the Father.

Jesus received and demonstrated the ministry of the Holy Spirit in order that He might impart it to the body of Christ through the baptism of the Holy Spirit. The same ministry in which Jesus operated has been deposited in His body. *"There are diversities of gifts, but the same Spirit. *There are differences of ministries, but the same Lord. *And there are diversities of activities, but it is the same God who works all in all"* (1 Corinthians 12:4-6). Jesus operated in the spiritual dimension with all of His spiritual senses in full operation. He had spirit eyes, ears, heart, and voice, which enabled Him to attack the Enemy on the Enemy's own ground. The sons of God must operate on this same level with all spiritual senses in operation in order to combat the Enemy on his ground. It is essential for the sons of God to seek the full restoration of their spiritual senses. How can we walk in obedience if we don't have a spiritual ear? How can we speak the word of God if we do not have a spiritual voice? How can we attack the Enemy if we don't have a spiritual eye? *"He who has an ear, let him hear what the Spirit says to the churches"* (Revelation 2:29).

In our own abilities and strength, we are not able to meet the tremendous needs that are in the world today. From experience I learned that my resources are not sufficient to produce life. God is looking for vessels that will allow Him to flow through them to meet the needs of the multitudes. The church of today is weak and anemic because men are preaching out of their own resources. We hear beautiful sermons but see very little life and very little edification for spiritual growth. Jesus wants to touch through us, speak through us, and manifest His glory through us. *"It is the Spirit who gives life; the flesh profits nothing. The words that I speak to you are spirit, and they are life"* (John 6:63).

Jesus went into the highways and byways preaching kingdom culture. Jesus cast out devils and established His new rule. He didn't go to the churches or synagogues to get recognized or for credentials; rather, He went to the lost sheep of the tribe of Israel. God's sons need to seek affirmation from our heavenly Father and not from men. When God's sons come out of the four walls and begin to imitate Jesus and cast out devils, then we will see real results. I have noticed how many modern Christians despise street preaching and the deliverance ministry. When I preached on the streets, in the jails, in homes, and in foreign countries, there is a much more powerful anointing than in the churches. People who have never actually experienced organic, raw street ministry are the biggest critics. They need to get out of the church pews before they start stinking!

I felt the call of Jesus to speak through me and to minister His Word through me. I understood that I needed to get out of the way and let Jesus have His way. When I first began to pastor on the reservation, I was confronted with tremendous overwhelming needs. I gave everything I had to help those in need, but it was only a drop in a bucket compared to what was needed. I cried out to the Lord for help, and the Spirit spoke to me: *"Let me be God, and you preach My Word."* It was amazing to see God move in behalf of people of faith!

The anointing and life-giving Word flows through vessels that have been enabled by the Holy Spirit to do the works of YHWH. Just as Creator gave His agent Adam the power of the spoken word, believers have also been given the creative power of the spoken word. God is looking for men and women whose hearts have been molded, whose minds have been transformed, and whose will have been conformed to His will. He is making us ministers of the Spirit. "...*but our sufficiency is from God, *[6]*who also made us sufficient as ministers of the new covenant, not of the letter but of the Spirit; for the letter kills, but the Spirit gives life*" (2 Corinthians 3:5).

THE EDIFYING OF THE BODY OF CHRIST

*"And He gave some, apostles; and some, prophets; and some, evangelists; and some, pastors and teachers; *[12]*For the perfecting of the saints, for the work of the ministry, for the edifying of the body of Christ: *[13]*Till we all come to the unity of the faith, and of the knowledge of the Son of God, unto a perfect man, unto the measure of the stature of the fulness of Christ."*
(Ephesians 4:11, KJV)

The body of Christ is in terrible need of edification in the day in which we live. The body of Christ is literally starving spiritually. The fivefold ministry has been given to the body of Christ for its edification and perfection, so it is essential that each ministry brings its full measure of edification to the body. The Holy Spirit gave me a vision of the church and what I saw was deformed midgets, sitting in the pews while the preacher was preaching. This is not a pretty picture but pretty well sums up the spiritual condition the church has produced. To *edify* means "*to impart spiritual nourishment that will build up and energize.*" For too long, the body of Christ has been under the control of the church, and the spirit of religion has stifled the work of God. Men stand behind the pulpit and preach out of their own intellect. "*These are spots in your love feasts ... clouds without water, carried about by the winds ...*" (Jude 12).

God gave Jesus a human body to do the works of the ministry, but now He has given Him the body of Christ to do His works. Just as Jesus operated in the fivefold ministry two thousand years ago, these same gifts operate in the body of Christ today. The fivefold ministry is the manifestation of the Holy Spirit operating through vessels that have been enabled for the ministry. The mantle of the Holy Spirit upon men and women of God is the manifestation of the life of King Jesus Himself. The fivefold ministry is the uniting of God and man in a ministry that will do His works. *"For we are His workmanship, created in Christ Jesus for good works, which God prepared beforehand that we should walk in them"* (Ephesians 2:10).

Many pastors and ministers fear change away from organized church structure into a more organic family-of-God model. The fear may be that it would in some way stifle the fivefold ministry; however, I believe it would be the opposite. As an evangelist for more than half of my ministry, I have found pastors, churches and denominations to be overprotective and closed off to Holy Spirit ministry. With the more organic movement of the family of God, prophets and evangelists would be free to be led by the Holy Spirit and homes and small groups would be open to receive them. Cities and communities would be in need of teaching and training; apostles and teachers would be in demand. Citywide revivals would be possible with small groups to receive new converts. The apostle Paul demonstrated this model at Ephesus where one of the greatest revivals broke out, *"... the word of the Lord grew mightily and prevailed"* (Acts 19:20). First, Paul found some disciples, convinced them and then empowered them with the Holy Spirit. When he met opposition from the church, he withdrew to the school of Tyrannus where he taught for two years. From there, the movement spread throughout the whole region.

Ministers are uncomfortable with disorder, and an organic movement may seem like chaos; however, we need to trust God and the moving of the Holy Spirit. Also, God will raise up men who will give direction, and the Holy Spirit will operate in the body of Christ to provide structure. Is it a foreign idea to put YHWH in charge of His own movement?

Through my experience, I have learned that the anointing comes by getting close to Jesus. The closer you get, the more powerful the anointing. The anointing emanates from Jesus, and I have learned that to get close to Jesus, you have to "pray through." That is an old-fashioned concept of praying until you press through the obstacles of the flesh, bring your mind and spirit into subjection until you touch Jesus. The longer you are in His presence, the more anointing you will operate in. Our daily lives bring all kinds of distractions and the Enemy majors on trying to divert our attention. This requires God's ministers to set priorities, and those who make Jesus their priority will discover that Jesus makes them His priority. I have been in meetings where the anointing is so strong you can smell it. I have also been in meetings where the anointing is so strong, it feels like electricity in the air; you can hear it crackle in the spiritual realm.

From the time I became a new Christian, I remember being in spiritual warfare of one sort or another. I was born again and baptized in the Holy Spirit in the fires of revival on my reservation. A Canadian Cree evangelist who had just completed a forty-day fast was holding a revival at the community center, and I accidentally attended the meeting, thinking it was the American Indian movement. There I surrendered my life to Jesus! As he was preaching the Word, I could feel it hit me. My spirit was saying, "Yes, yes, this is what I need."

A big part of that revival was learning how to "pray through"; that is, praying until you broke through the flesh and laid hold of the horns of the altar. You prayed until the glory came down. One thing I learned from my Cree brother, for which I am grateful, is learning how to pray through before preaching. When we got to church, we knelt down and prayed in the Spirit until it was time to minister. Every day we would kneel down in his motel room and pray until we touched Jesus. In the early years, I sat under many very good Holy Ghost evangelists; finally, God placed me in a church where I sat under an anointed pastor. One of the teachings my pastor stressed was that we are the highest authority. From our position seated in heavenly places, we have the authority in the spiritual realm over principalities and powers. He taught me that when I came to town, the demons trembled. On the reservations, there is plenty of opportunity to wage spiritual warfare.

In those early years, casting out demons was a big part of the ministry. We may not have done it right and it may not have been very pretty, but we were waging war against the powers of the Enemy. I always say, "The demons on the reservation aren't embarrassed; they just kinda hang out where everyone can see them. The big difference with the white man is that they know how to hide their demons."

When I was a young pastor, I remember well when a drunken man came off the streets into the church to challenge us with his spiritual powers. He was a well-known medicine man in the community and always carried a set of deer hoofs from which he claimed he obtained magical powers. He came to the front of the church, chanting and shaking his deer hoofs. To his surprise, I asked, *"May I look at your magic hooves?"*

He handed them to me, I walked briskly to the door, ran outside and threw them as far as I could. When I walked back in, he was astonished. I asked him, *"Where is your power now?"* He hung his head and staggered out the way he came in.

Young pastors had to learn how to deal with demonic oppression with love and authority. One time a rowdy drunk came into my church and began disrupting the service. I had two big strong Indian men in the church, and I said, *"Les, stand up. Alphonse, stand up."* I looked at the man being disruptive and said, *"Brother, sit down and shut up or I will have these two men throw you out of the church."* He sat down! Eventually he got saved and demons cast out. I'm sure we all have many experiences we could share. I have always said, *"If someone is serious about being in the ministry, he must spend at least one year on a reservation."*

When God's children grasp the significance of, ministering in Christ and by the Holy Spirit, they realize it is His ministry. It is Him who is preaching and healing, and teaching and working miracles. However, most Christians don't even know the names of God. Satan is not only the father of lies but is also the master deceiver who veils the truth from blinded Christians. One of the most important truths the Devil has hidden is that he does not exist, and another is the proper name of God. The world has been conditioned to believe that His name is God. When referring to Creator God or referring to our Creator deity, Christians use the noun *God* for His name. Why do they call Him *God?* Because they do not know His proper name! The word *god* is a noun and refers to a deity, which could probably refer to, Gad, or Allah or any number of deities in the world. In India, where millions of gods are worshipped, at least the people have the respect to call them by their proper names, e.g., *Shiva.* Calling Him *God* is like calling your friend *man* instead of their proper name. A *noun* is "a person, place, or thing"— not a proper name. In the King James Version of the Bible and most translations, the proper name of God cannot be found. Why could this be? The sons of God will know their Daddy's name and have it written in their hearts and on their foreheads. True sovereignty knows the proper name of God. There can be no relationship if we do not know someone's name.

CHAPTER 12

WHAT IS GOD'S NAME?

"I am the LORD [YHWH], *that is My name;*
and My glory I will not give to another..."
(Isaiah 42:8)

THE PROPER NAMES OF God have been hidden from the
world but is now being revealed to the *family of YHWH*. It has
been said that the Old Testament is Jesus concealed, but
the New Testament is Jesus revealed. I think this saying could be
changed to appropriately say, *"The Old Testament is the name of God
revealed, but the New Testament is the name of God concealed"*.
We are privileged to be living in an age where disclosure of
His name is being given to His chosen, *"No one knows the Son
but the Father, nor does anyone know the Father except the Son
and the one to whom the Son wills to reveal Him."* (Matthew
16: 13-17). The apostle Paul's discovery of *"the altar to the
unknown God"* is once again relevant to our generation:
*"...Therefore, the One whom you worship without knowing,
Him I proclaim to you!"* (Acts 17:23). If you have arrived at this
page, you should be very happy and blessed at what you are about
to read.

Does God have a name? If so, why has it been hidden
from us? And if He does, why has the name of God been
completely eliminated from the vernacular of modern
civilization? The answer to the first question is an emphatic

"Yes"! God does have a name, and His name is clearly revealed to us—from the book of Genesis to the end of Revelation. He is the Creator and possessor of heaven and earth; the original architect and sole owner of all things and man can know the name of God if he searches the Word of God with an open heart and allows the Holy Spirit to give him understanding. God revealed His name to Moses on Mount Sinai as "YHWH." The proper name, YHWH, called the Tetragrammaton, is used over 6700 times in the Jewish *Tanakh*.

For many years, I questioned why modern Bible translators never used God's proper name, and why they substituted the title *LORD*? One of my pastors told me everywhere you see the word LORD capitalized it represents the name of God, that put a question in my heart? The name of God never appeared in the Bible; "*Why would they do that*? When reading modern Bible translations references to the supreme deity is, *The LORD, LORD God Almighty, The LORD of Hosts, God*, or *Almighty God*, but never is He addressed by His proper name. The importance of knowing someone's name is relationship; there can be no relationship if you don't know the person's name! The omission of God's proper name from the human conscience can only lead us to conclude that this is one of the greatest deceptions in human history. My discovery of this cover-up started me on a journey to find the proper name of God—*THE NAME THAT IS ABOVE ALL NAMES!*

THE KING OF THE UNIVERSE DEMOTED

From 1604 to 1611, scholars were commissioned by King James I to translate the Bible into English. The King James translators were committed to producing an English Bible that would be a more accurate translation. However, these Bible translators were faced with a dilemma; they were afraid to assign a higher title to Jesus than that of King James of

England. The translators were afraid a higher title for Jesus would offend the king, so they substituted a title— "*LORD*"— instead of using God's proper name. The title of *LORD* is a lower level of hierarchy in English aristocracy than a *king* or *duke*, but the supreme title of *king* was exclusively reserved for King James I of England. English translators hid the name YHWH by replacing it with the title, LORD! A good practice for believers is to replace LORD, with the name YHWH in their Bibles. The word *lord* is defined as "an aristocrat, a nobleman, and a member of the aristocracy." Have you heard of the "House of Lords"? It is made up of the rich elite aristocracy of England. The lords originated from the rich British landlords who were property owners in Europe. Remember the verse, "Ten lords a leaping" in the song "The Twelve Days of Christmas"? This song illustrates the relatively low estate of European lords. The irony is they assigned the title of Lord to the King of the Universe, effectively removing God's name from the consciousness of man. I think the Devil chuckles every time we quote Philippians 2:11 "*and that every tongue should confess that Jesus Christ is Lord…*"

THE NAME OF CREATOR DISCLOSED

The original name of Creator God was disclosed to Moses at the burning bush. "…*The LORD God* [YHWH] *of your fathers, the God of Abraham, the God of Isaac, and the God of Jacob, has sent me unto you. This is My name forever, and this is My memorial to all generations*" (Exodus 3:15). The Hebrew name of God, *YHWH*, called the Tetragrammaton, was translated into English as LORD. This translation was erroneous! Instead, the Hebrew name *YHWH* should have been translated into English as "*YHWH*." In Biblical theology, *YHWH*, the name of God is called the Tetragrammaton; the Three are one in name and in substance, co-substantial, omnipotent, omnipresent, omniscient, they are of one mind, one will and all share in the heavenly lovefest with their family (the Agapeo), the Godhead bodily. In announcing His proper name to Moses, *YHWH* affirmed His relationship to the tribe of Hebrews by announcing He was the same deity who had made covenant with Abraham, Isaac, and Jacob. The name of God, "*YHWH,*" was established forever. Moses was reluctant to announce the new name to the Israelites, since they had not retained His name during the captivity and only knew Him as, *El Shaddi,* (Exodus 6:3). Moses asked YHWH God what he should tell the children of Israel when they ask, "What is his name".

> ... *"When I come to the children of Israel and say to them, 'The God of your fathers has sent me to you,' and they say to me, 'What is His name?' what shall I say to them?"* [14] *And God said to Moses, "I AM WHO I AM [HAYAH]." And He said, "Thus you shall say to the children of Israel, 'YHWH has sent me to you.'"* [15] *Moreover God said to Moses, "Thus you shall say to the children of Israel: "The LORD [YHWH] God of your fathers, the God of Abraham, the God of Isaac, and the God of Jacob, has sent me to you..."* (Exodus 3:13-15).

In this particular statement, God is speaking in the first person and calls Himself, "HAYAH," but He then commands Moses to tell the children of Israel that YHWH has sent Me to you. The reason we don't call Him *HAYAH* is because it is a first-person reference. YHWH would be the second or third-person reference, which is appropriate for us to use. For instance, I can refer to myself as, "I am," but it is not proper for you to call me "I am"; you would say, "You are" or "He is."

Most English theologians identify *Hayah* as "I AM WHO I AM" or "the eternal or self-existent one." Modern Christians when asked, "What is the name of God?" would commonly say, "I AM who I AM." However, under closer examination, the Hebrew verb *Hayah* is an emphatic declaration; a better interpretation can be found in God's word at the creation. In Genesis 1:3, God decrees *hayah* or *"Let there be,"* and there was. The Hebrew verb *Hayah* when spoken is the creative word of YHWH and reveals to us how everything was fashioned from the invisible by His spoken word. The New Testament equivalent *is* found in John 1:1-3, *the* Greek word logos: *"In the beginning was the Word [Logos], and the Word [Logos] was with God, and the Word [Logos] was God. ²He was in the beginning with God. ³All things were made through Him, and without Him nothing was made that was made."* Logos is the Greek equivalent of the Hebrew verb *Hayah*.

Moses continued to question God, *"... suppose they will not believe me or listen to my voice?"* (Exodus 4:1) YHWH replied, *"... What is that in your hand?"* (v. 2a) Moses replied, *"A rod"* (v. 2b) YHWH explained to Moses that the rod would be the point of contact and would release the dynamics of His authority showing signs and wonders that would convince the naysayers. Moses and his brother Aaron gathered the elders of Israel, and spoke all the words YHWH had given them. The Bible says, *"So the people believed..."* (Exodus 4:31).

Afterward Moses went to Pharaoh and announced, *"...Thus says YHWH God of Israel: 'Let My people go...'"* (Exodus 5:1). Pharaoh's reaction to Moses' declaration is interesting; he replies: *"Who is YHWH, that I should obey His voice ... I do not know YHWH..."* (v. 2). Pharaoh's reaction is comparable to the reaction people have when we share the name YHWH for the first time; it is totally foreign to them: "Who is YHWH? We don't know YHWH." In fact, this is the same reaction Christians have when they hear the proper name of God for the first time, "Who is YHWH?" The proper name of God is totally alien to the modern-day church.

MAKE HIS NAME KNOWN

The elimination of the name of God from modern vernacular was a carefully crafted scheme conceived by the master deceiver himself and propagated by the scribes and Pharisees. One of the ways he used to hide the name was through the traditions of Jews. The traditions of the Jews to never utter the name nor let it pass through their lip's is diabolically opposed to the spirit of the Word of God. This is the leaven of the Sadducees and Pharisees; we are commanded throughout the Word of God to glorify His name and to exalt His name in the entire world. YHWH God charged Moses to make His name known.

> *And God spoke to Moses and said to him, "I am the LORD* [YHWH]. *³I appeared to Abraham, to Isaac, and to Jacob, as God Almighty* [El Shaddai], *but by My name LORD* [YHWH] *I was not known to them. ⁴I have also established My covenant with them … ⁶Therefore say to the children of Israel:* '*I am the LORD* [YHWH]'; *I will bring you out from under the burdens of the Egyptians, I will rescue you from their bondage, and I will redeem you with an outstretched arm and with great judgments. ⁷I will take you as My people, and I will be your God. Then you shall know that I am the LORD* [YHWH] *your God who brings you out from under the burdens of the Egyptians … ⁸I am YHWH"'* (Exodus 6:2-8).

The charge to make His name known to the nations is a constant theme throughout the Bible, and is contrary to the traditions of the Jews who don't ever allow the enemy to muffle your voice and stop you from glorifying the God of all creation. The elimination of the name of God is leaven of the Pharisees and Sadducees. A good exercise to become accustomed to the name YHWH is to read through the books of Psalms and Isaiah and insert the name YHWH wherever the title LORD is used.

PRONUNCIATION OF THE NAME

(יהוה) The inscription on the left is the Modern Hebrew spelling of YHWH. Notice that the Hebrew language reads right to left, but when we write it in English, it is left to right, so YHWH is the correct English spelling. The correct pronunciation of the name is the phonetic sound of the letters which are all consonants; "Y" or *yod*, "H" or *hey*, "W" or *wah*, "H" or *hey*; <u>Yod Hey Wah Hey</u>. The ancient 22-letter Paleo- Hebrew language assigned a pronunciation for each letter of their alphabet, assigned a numerical value to each letter, and in addition, a meaning.

"Y" = *yod* = "the hand" = 10
"H" = *hey* = "behold" or "look" = 5
"W" = *wah* = "nail" = 6
"H" = *hey* = "behold" = 5

The name is *"Yod Hey Wah Hey"* or in English *"Behold the Hand, Behold the Nail"*

NAMES HAVE MEANING

My search for the name of God has been over an extended number of years. I have read many teachings by Hebrew scholars and other learned theologians and teachers on His name, but, for some reason, my spirit was never fully satisfied with their explanations. A friend had given me a copy of the Paleo alphabet, and I was sitting at my desk, copying the letters and the meaning of each letter. "Boom!" It hit me! The Holy Spirit unfolded the pronunciation of the letters of the Tetragrammaton and His interpretation, and what I discovered exploded in my spirit as a jaw-dropping revelation. The tingling presence of the Holy Spirit flowed from the top of my head to the pit of my stomach. In my spirit, Yod Hey Wah Hey whispered, *"This is my name."* My first thought was, *could this really be? This is so simple! How could we have missed this for so long?* The western mind and modern reasoning somehow missed the heart of YHWH God and the revelation of His identity. The simple name, YOD HEY WAH HEY, contains the revelation of His heart for all humanity and His redemptive purpose: "BEHOLD THE HAND, BEHOLD THE NAIL."

WE KNOW HIM BY HIS NAME

My Native American heritage helped me grasp the simplicity of the name. The Blackfeet language is a compilation of phonetic sounds combined to make words and phrases; each phonic sound has a meaning or an interpretation. On the other hand, in English the letters are simply the sounds of letters and names without meaning. Several years ago, I was honored with my Blackfeet name, *Ee Doh Moh.* The English interpretation of my name is *"He is the One Who Leads the Warriors into Battle, or War Chief."* I am a Vietnam veteran and a minister of the gospel and my Indian name is not simply a word; it is the definition of who I am. Someone said that God's name is rich in meaning and revelation, and as we are introduced to His name we are introduced to His character. God always begins a relationship by revealing His name [just as we do], which in turn reveals His nature and His attitude toward them. When God gives us His name, He is telling us who He wants to be to us. Becoming intimately engaged in His name ignites your heart to worship Him.

DO NOT ADD TO OR TAKE AWAY

The rational mind seeks to pronounce the Tetragrammaton as a whole word instead of pronouncing each letter, which has resulted in hybrid and inaccurate names. The Hebrew language actually uses the letter "V" instead of the "W," but pronounces the "V" with the "uah" sound. So instead of *Vah*, they would say *uah*. Notice the two small marks at the bottom of the larger Hebrew letters; these are vowel marks. The vowel marks were added to the Hebrew alphabet around the seventh century AD by a group of Hebrew scholars called the Masorettes who introduced the system of vowel points[25]; however, the ancient Paleo alphabet did not use vowel marks. But how can you pronounce a name that does not have vowels? Therefore, to make it more palatable to the western mindset they added the vowel marks. That is where hybrid names like *Yahweh, Yahwah, Jehovah, Yahovah,* and *Yahuah* were derived. There is a myriad of teachings on the pronunciations, but the fact that the ancient Paleo language did not use vowel marks negates all of their rational arguments. The problem with these names is that they do not reveal the heart of God or His plan of redemption. It is so simple that the wise have omitted the name of God from the entire Bible and have forgotten His commandment, " *You shall not add to the word* [especially the name of God!] *which I command you, nor take from it …*" (Deuteronomy 4:2; see also Revelation 22:19). The simplicity of pronouncing the letters of the name, YHWH *(Yod Hey Wah Hey)*, is profound and confounds the rational mind because it not only reveals who God is, but also the plan of redemption from the beginning to the end. *Yod Hey Wah Hey* is the Lamb of God who was slain from before the foundation of the world.

THE OMISSION OF THE NAME

One can deduce that early Christian translators acceded to the traditions of the Jews whose custom was never to speak the name of YHWH they believed that the name

---

25   "Hebrew Word Studies," www.logosapostolic.org, accessed 17 June 2016

was too holy to be uttered by sinful lips and should never be pronounced as it is spelled. The proper name, YHWH, was eventually replaced in Jewish worship with *Hashem* or *Adonai*, which are not actual names but titles. During prayer, or when a blessing is recited, or when a Torah verse is read the four-letter name YHWH, which appears over 6700 times in the Torah, is pronounced as *Adonai*, the Hebrew title meaning "God who is Master of All." At other times, the name YHWH is pronounced as *Hashem*, which literally means, "The Name"[26]; however, in doing a word study the word Hashem has more diabolical roots, Ashora, Hashema, etc. *Adonai* and *Hashem* are more suitable as titles for a deity, but not as a proper name. The omission of the name *Yod Hey Wah Hey* by Bible translators opened the door for the powers of darkness to undermine religious traditions and concealed the name of God.

GOD'S PROPER NAME

When I go to Western-style churches, it is unbearably sterile to hear the preachers talk about "God." They use the noun *god*, as if it is our Creator's name. You hear them extolling the name "Gaaada" time and time again, but they have no clue He has a proper name. nor do they realize that Gad is an ancient name of a false deity. "God" is not His proper name; God is what He is. *YOD HEY WAH HEY* is His name, and that is what we should call Him.

YHWH OMITTED FROM THE NEW TESTAMENT

In transition from the Old to the New Testament, we suddenly see the name YHWH omitted from the writings

---

26 Rabbi Nosson Scherman, Ed., Tanach the Stone edition, XXV (Brooklyn: Mesorah Publications, Ltd., 1996).

of the apostles. Are we to assume that the Holy Spirit neglected to use the name YHWH, or can we infer another more sinister plot perpetuated by a more sinister being and associates? Under closer inspection, we see that in fact, the apostles did use the name of YHWH, and Jesus emphatically taught them the name. The question is, who and when was the name YHWH omitted from New Testament writing?

Jesus taught the name, *YOD HEY WAH HEY*, to the apostles. He ardently believed it was essential to reveal the name of the Father and His character to the apostles. *"And this is eternal life, that they may know You, the only true God, and Jesus Christ whom You have sent"* (John 17:3). Jesus was emphatic about the apostles knowing the name. From His teaching and preaching we can deduce that not only did Jesus disclose the name, but He declared it to them and manifested it to them.

> John 17:6, *"I have <u>manifested Your name</u> to the men whom You have given Me out of the world…"*

> John17:11, *"… Holy Father, <u>keep through Your name</u> those whom You have given Me…"*

> John 17:12, *"While I was with them in the world, I <u>kept them in Your name</u> …"*

> John 17:26, *"And I have <u>declared to them Your name</u> …"*

From these verses we can deduce that Jesus regularly used the name "YHWH" in His preaching and teaching. For instance, when Jesus was asked, *"… which is the great commandment in the law?" ³⁷He said to him, "'You shall love the LORD [YHWH] your God with all your heart, with all your soul, and with all your mind"* (Mathew 22:36, 37). This is a direct quote from Deuteronomy 6:5, but a more accurate interpretation is; *"You shall love Yod Hey Wah Hey your God with all your heart, with all your soul, and with all your mind."* Don't you think that using the word Lord is very generic in a verse as important is this one?

Jesus quoted directly from the original Hebrew Scriptures, which would have used the Tetragrammaton before it was changed by Jewish scribes. In the latter part of this chapter Jesus asked the Pharisees, *"... How then does David in the Spirit call Him 'LORD* [YHWH],*' saying: ⁴⁴'The LORD* [*YHWH*] *said to my Lord [Adonai], sit at My right hand, Till I make Your enemies Your footstool?"* (Matthew 22:44). Jesus again quoted the Hebrew prophets in Luke 4:18, which says, *"The Spirit of the LORD* [*YHWH*] *is upon Me, because He has anointed Me to preach the gospel to the poor... ¹⁹To proclaim the acceptable year of the LORD* [*YHWH*].*"* I don't think Isaiah used the word, Lord. These are just a few scriptures to prove that the name, *Yod Hey Wah Hey*, was a regular part of Jesus' teaching and this brings us to the next question; which is, did the apostles use God's proper name?

THE APOSTLES KNEW THE NAME

The apostles knew the name of YHWH. As devout Jews, they were all taught the name in the synagogue, so the apostles were well-schooled in the name of the God. After the Holy Spirit fell on the disciples in the upper room the apostle Peter stood up and declared, *"And it shall come to pass that whoever calls on the name of the LORD* [Yod Hey Wah Hey] *shall be saved"* (Acts 2:21). Then speaking under the inspiration of the Holy Spirit, he says, *'The LORD* [Yod Hey Wah Hey] *said to my Lord* [Adonai], *"Sit at My right hand, till I make Your enemies Your footstool"* (Acts 2:35).

Throughout the book of Acts, the apostles used the name YHWH. In fact, the apostle Paul, a student of Gamaliel, was well-schooled in the Pharisaic tradition and was intimately knowledgeable of the name makes reference to it in Ephesians, declaring that the whole family of God is named *Yod Hey Wah Hey*. *"For this reason, I bow my knees to the Father [YHWH] of our Lord Jesus Christ, *[15]*from whom the whole family in heaven and earth is named"* (Ephesians 3:14, 15).

The apostles were commissioned by Jesus to go make disciples of all nations baptizing them in the name of the Father, the Son, and the Holy Spirit (Matthew 28:19). They were specifically commanded to use the name *YOD HEY WAH HEY* in water baptism. When you are given power of attorney to act in someone's name, you don't say, "I come in the name." No, you use the specific proper name of the person who has empowered you: "I baptize you in the name of the Father *(Yod Hey Wah Hey)*, and the name of the Son, Jesus *(Yahshua)*, and the Holy Spirit *(EliYah)*." Notice the name *EliYah, the proper name of the Holy Spirit* is used for the first time in this book. I believe Holy Spirit has a name that is being disclosed as well as the name of Yahshua.

DISCLOSURE OF THE NAME TO HIS CHOSEN

Jesus emphatically declared the name *Yod Hey Wah Hey* to the apostles, who carried the name into the entire world as they preached the Gospel. Jesus said,

> *"... I thank You, Father, Lord of heaven and earth, that You have hidden these things from the wise and prudent and have revealed them to babes. *[26]*Even so, Father, for so it seemed good in Your sight. *[27]*All things have been delivered to me by My Father, and no one knows the Son except the Father. Nor does anyone know the Father except the Son, and the one to whom the Son wills to reveal Him"* (Matthew 11:25-27).

It is apparent then that knowing the Father, the Son and the Holy Spirit is exclusively disclosed only to His chosen, *"And they shall be mine says YHWH of hosts in that day that day that I make them my jewels."* (Malachi 3:17). We, who are a party to the family of God, have been shown great favor in knowing Him. Knowing Him, then, is not just as a casual acquaintance, but in an intimate, face-to-face relationship, including knowing His name. As I have already mentioned, God always begins a relationship with a person by revealing His name, just as we do, which in turn reveals His nature and His attitude toward them. When God discloses to us a name by which He desires to be called, He is telling us who He wants to be to us.

Yahshua HaNasaret WeMalek HaYudah

The declaration of the true identity of Jesus was openly disclosed to the whole world at His crucifixion. *"Now Pilate wrote a title and put it on the cross. And the writing was: JESUS OF NAZARETH, THE KING OF THE JEWS ... [20] and it was written in Hebrew, Greek and Latin* (John 19:19, 20). The chief priest and Pharisees objected vehemently. Why? Because they saw that the first letter in each of the words in the Hebrew inscription, *Yahshua Hanasarat WeMalek HeYudah,* spelled "YHWH." When the Jews read the inscription, they were stunned and scrambled to cover it up and asked Pilot to remove it realizing the identity of Whom they had crucified. Pilot answered, "it is what it is". Jesus declared, *"... He who has seen Me has seen the Father..."* (John 14:9). The writing on the cross was written in three languages, the Hebrew is as follows:

Jesus — *Yahshua* — "Y" — *Yod* — "Hand"
of Nazareth — *Hanasarat* — "H" — *Hey* — "Behold"
The King — *WeMalik* — "W" — *Wah* — "Nail"
of Judah — *HeYudah* — "H" — *Hey* — "Behold"

The inscription miraculously disclosed that Jesus is indeed the Hebrew God of Creation. Remember the letters interpreted are: "Y" — *Yod* — "the hand"; "H" — *Hey* — "behold"; "W" — *Wah* — "nail"; "H" — *Hey* — "behold." So, YHWH from the beginning was the Lamb slain from before the foundations of the world, and He physically manifested the name in His flesh on the cross, ***Behold the Hand, Behold the Nail.*** There are many depictions of Jesus, and He even said that many would come in His name, but we will know His true identity when we see Him—by the nail scars in His hands and feet.

WHO IS YHSWH

The name of Jesus is an interesting study. The original Hebrew birth name given to Him was YAHSHUA or in English we say Joshua. The Greek interpreters did not have the letter Y in their alphabet and changed His name to Iesus, pronounced, eye ee sus. Iesus was the standard name used for twelve hundred years until the British translators interpreted the Bible in the fifteenth and sixteenth centuries. The English translators inserted the letter J instead of the Y and gave us the name of Jesus. The name of Jesus is relatively new and has only been in use for about five hundred years. Some scholars believe this name is a reference to Zeus, however, I am not ready to go there.

In the book of Revelation 3:12 Jesus speaks about His new name. For the longest time I was expecting the Holy Spirit to reveal a new name to us, however, as I was praying one day, I asked YHWH, *"Please, please tell me what is the new name of Jesus"*? He said, *"Jesus"!* I was stunned and asked Him, *Why Jesus?* He said, *"Jesus is His new name, His birth name is Yahshua"*. Wow, that goes to show how small minded we are. Yahshua has been here a long time and Jesus is a new comer. This caused me to wonder if the name Jesus was acceptable to him since I was saved by the name of Jesus as well as millions of others. Holy Spirit assured me this is okay. Jesus has accepted it and calls it His new name and we can be comforted in our salvation.

The Hebrew name Yahshua is made of two words, Yah and shua; Yah is the ancient name of YHWH and shua means God is salvation. The interpretation of His name is, "Yah is salvation". The Hebrew spelling of Yahshua is YHSWH. Does that look familiar? Yud Hey Shin Wah Hey. The Hebrew letter in the middle is Shin meaning to chew, crush, destroy, revealing the judgment Yahshua endured when He was crushed for our salvation, *"Surely He has born our griefs and carried our sorrows; Yet we esteemed Him stricken, smitten of God and afflicted, but He was crushed for our transgressions, He was bruised for our iniquities; the chastisement of our peace was upon Him, and by His wounds I am healed."* (Isaiah 53:4, 5).

There is another name that no one knows but is being revealed to those who He wills to reveal. Revelation 19:12 describes a triumphant warrior King Jesus seated on a white horse with a name written that no one knows but He Himself. The name isn't King of Kings and Lord of Lord's because these are titles and not names. The name is in plain sight and Jesus clearly calls Himself by the name but for some reason nobody associates the name with Him. He says it's a new name but it is also an old name. This name is in the original Hebrew writing but has been removed from English Bibles more than ten thousand times, according to the Strongs Concordance.

Jesus calls Himself by the name four times, Revelations 1:8 vs11 and 21:6, 22:13; **"I am Alep/Tav"**! The Greek interpreted the Aleph/Tav as Alpha and Omega but I don't believe Jesus was speaking to the Apostle John in Greeks. The Aleph is the first letter in the Paleo Hebrew alphabet meaning the head man or a strong leader and the Tav is the last letter in their alphabet, meaning, a cross, a covenant, a symbol or sign. The Aleph/Tav are symbolic of the entire Hebrew alphabet from which God spoke the word and the heavens and the earth were created. It is found twice in the first sentence of the Bible, Genesis 1:1 *"In the beginning God created the heavens and the earth."* In the original Hebrew text, it reads as follows, *"Berishete bara Elohim Aleph/Tav samayim Aleph/Tav erets"*. In English it reads, *"In the beginning created God Aleph/Tav the heavens Aleph/Tav the earth."* Another place it is used is in Isaiah 6:1 *"In the year King Uzziah died I also saw the Lord sitting upon a throne, high and lifted up."* In English, *"I saw also Aleph/Tav Adonia sitting upon a throne."* One of my favorite places it is used is in Isaiah 53:6, *"And the Lord has laid on Him the iniquity of us all."* In English, *"And YHWH has laid on Him Aleph/Tav the iniquity of us all."* Time and space prevent me from listing the more than ten thousand times Aleph/Tav is used in the Old Testament but we will speak more on this in the last chapter, Time is Short.

THE NAME of HOLY SPIRIT REVEALED

The Bible tells us plainly what the name of Holy Spirit is in Isaiah 9:6! *"And His name will be called wonderful, councilor, **Almighty God.**"* The words wonderful and councilor can be taken as adjectives but the name given to us is Almighty God. The Jews call Him Ruach Ho Kadesh; Ruach meaning breath or spirit and Kadesh means holy, consecrated sacred; however, this is a description not a name. Jesus said, *"And if you are willing to receive it, He is Elijah who is to come"* (Matthew 11:14). Elijah is two Hebrew words, Eli and Yah; El is an ancient name for the supreme deity and Yah is the ancient name for God almighty. The double reference to Almighty God emphasizes the significance. Jesus used a double reference to the name Almighty God when he cried out on the cross, "Eli, Eli ... My God, My God," (Matthew 27:46 and Psalm 22:1). In Malachi 4:5 *"Behold, I will send you Elijah the prophet."* I don't think

He was saying that He was going to resurrect Elijah from his sky home but He was speaking of another entity that the name belonged to. Jesus made the same type of reference to John the Baptist in Matthew 11:14 *"And if you are willing to receive it, he is Elijah who is to come, he who has ears to hear, let him hear."* This is an important spiritual concept if you are to enter into spiritual prophetic revelation. He was not referring to the physical fleshly man John the Baptist, but to the Spirit that was upon him. God sees the spirit not the flesh, *"God is Spirit, and those who worship Him must worship in Spirit and truth"* (John 4:24). "Holy Spirits proper name is "EliYah. You will see the importance of knowing their names when we come to Water Baptism.

GOD'S IDENTITY DISCLOSED

In the gospel of John 20:19-30, after Jesus had been buried, the confused and mourning disciples gathered together, when, without any warning, Jesus appeared to them. His first act was to show them His hands and His side. His was not a random act but was calculated and highly significant because it disclosed His true identity to those who had gathered. This is something that no one in the world is privy to—only those to whom the Holy Spirit reveals. Thomas was not with those who had gathered, and when the others told him they had seen the Master, he declared, *"… Unless I see in His hands the prints of the nails, and put my hand into His side I will not believe"* (John 20:25).

Why would Thomas make such a declaration? Thomas had received the revelation of the name.

> *And after eight days … Jesus came, the doors being shut, and stood in the midst, and said, "Peace to you!"* [27] *Then he said to Thomas, "Reach your finger here, and look at My hands; and reach your hand here, and put it into My side. Do not be unbelieving but believing."* [28] *And Thomas answered*

and said to Him, "My Lord (YHWH) and my God!"
(John 20:26-28).

When Thomas saw the nail-scarred hands and the hole in Jesus' side, he knew that Jesus was in fact, *YOD HEY WAH HEY—* "BEHOLD THE HAND, BEHOLD THE NAIL." Jesus not only declared His identity, but He physically manifested the name in His body. Jesus was not simply a man; He was God in the flesh! This is how we will know Him! This is how we will identify Him! Many will come in His name, but we will know Him when we see Him by the nail scars in His hands and the piercing in His side. Jesus is *"YOD HEY WAH HEY."*

An important scripture that must be interpreted through Holy Spirit prophetic revelation is found in the book of Philippians 2:9-11, *"Therefore, God has highly exalted Him and given Him* **the Name** *which is above every name, that at the name of Jesus every knee shall bow … and that every tongue should confess that Jesus Christ is Lord to the glory of God the Father."* This is not a good interpretation of what YHWH wanted to express to His children, because He wants us to understand what He means by giving Jesus the **Name**. We must understand that the interpreters in the year 1511 were not Holy Spirit baptized men. These were men who had just come out of the reformation and the names of God had been obscured much like the children of Israel when Moses came with a new name. We have to give them credit for the good job they did but there are things that are highly significant that must be exposed. Allow me to give a new interpretation using the names of God that have been revealed to us. *Therefore, YHWH has highly exalted Yahshua and given Him* **the Name** *which is above every name, that at the name of YHWH every knee shall bow … and that every tongue should confess that Yahshua Ha Mashiach is YHWH to the glory of Yah the Father."* This revelation is highly important especially in light of what Jesus told us in Matthew 7:21 *"Not everyone who says to me, Lord, Lord, shall enter the Kingdom of heaven, but He who does the will of my Father in heaven. Many will come in that day and say, 'Lord, Lord, have we not prophesied in your name, cast out demons in Your name, and done many wonders in Your name?' And I will declare to them, 'I never knew you; depart from Me, you who practice lawlessness!"* I don't think Yahshua likes to be called Lord. It would behoove a whole lot of preachers and Christians to repent and fall on their faces confessing, we are sorry we have not known you or your name!

THE ONENESS OF GOD

With all of these names and all of the deceptions and confusion I have to bring you back to the basics and central revelation of who God really is; there is only one Elohim (GOD), **YHWH**! He is the Creator and possessor of heaven and earth; He is the original architect and sole owner of all creation. All of this is important because Yahshua is coming back for a people who have been sealed with the name of YHWH. Yahshua made the declaration in Mark 12:29 *"Hear O Israel, YHWH your God, YHWH is one, and you shall love YHWH with all of your heart, with all of your soul, with all of your mind, and with all your strength."* How can we love Him if we don't know His name? We must understand that YHWH is one God but has three manifestations, three faces. I call them the masks of God. He wears three masks but is the same person. I think one of the confusions is to refer to the Father exclusively, as YHWH; No, YHWH is the name of the one God and He is the Father, the Son, and Holy Spirit. He manifests Himself to creation in three masks, The Father, Yahshua (the Son), and EliYah (Holy Spirit).

A good illustration of the faces of God is given to us in the book of Ezekiel chapter 1:4-12 where Ezekiel had a vision of four beasts each having four faces; *"As for the likeness of their faces, each one had the face of a man; each of the four had the face of a lion on the right side, each had the face of an ox on the left side, and each of the four had the face of an eagle."* This seems incredible but it shows us that God is not a man but a being incredible beyond description. Ezekiel's angel was one being but he had four faces. For the believer to understand the holy Trinity we must understand that God is one being and His name is YHWH; however, He is one person and has three faces; He wears the face of the Father, we can call Him YHWH, He wears the face of the Son, Yahshua, and He wears the face of EliYah, the Holy Spirit.

The appearance of the Godhead is not easily grasped by the natural understanding of human nature since God is not man so His appearance is not human in the way He appears. Jesus said, *"I thank you Father, Yah of heaven and earth, that You have hidden these things from the wise and prudent and have revealed them unto babes … No one knows the Son except the Father, nor does anyone know the Father except the Son, and the one to whom He whom He wills to reveal Him,"* (Matthew 11:25-27). So, the revelation of the Godhead is only disclosed to the select children whom He chooses to bring into revelation knowledge of Him. As we discussed the angel with four faces in Ezekiel's revelation, chapter one, and the appearance of the beasts with four faces around the throne of God in Revelation five, these multi faced images are not a strange phenomenon in God's realm of existence. The appearance of the Trinity is that of a being with three faces; the face of the Father, the face of the Son, and the face of the Holy Spirit. When a human encounters one of the three manifestations of the Godhead they would only see one face as it would be the face of one of the three; for example, if one encounters Aleph/Tav Jesus they would only see the face of Jesus but all three would be present. When one encounters the glory of God, they are looking into the face of EliYah, Holy Spirit; for instance, when you pray and you feel the presence of God you are looking into the face of EliYah, Holy Spirit. When one encounters the presence of God in the heavenly teepee, Mount Zion, they could be encountering the face of the Father because He craves the presence of His children gathered around the campfire.

The holy Trinity is the figure of the "Three in One" with each face appearing in the Godhead. We should understand that each one of the Trinity are not bound or confined to one space as they are able to step out and manifest at their will since God is omnipotent, (all powerful), omnipresent, (or all present), omniscient, (all knowing), co-substantial, and He is all seeing. As we discussed the heavenly council fire where the three are conversing about creating mankind, you can imagine each of the three stepping out of the Godhead and gathering around the fire and having a face-to-face conversation. Scarface's encounter with the heavenly family was of the three gathered together in the heavenly teepee. I can think of no greater revelation of the heavenly family in all of scripture than that given to Scarface. It is hard to understand how early American Christians considered this to be a Pegan religion.

Satan is not only the father of lies but is also the master deceiver who veils the truth from blinded Christians. One of the most important truths the Devil has hidden is that he does not exist, and another is the proper names of God. The world has been conditioned to believe that His name is God. When referring to Creator God or referring to the Creator deity, Christians use the noun *God* for His name. Why would they call Him *God*? Because they do not know His proper name! The word *god* is a noun and refers to a deity, which could probably refer to "Allah" or any number of deities in the world. In India where millions of gods are worshipped the people at least have the respect to call them by their proper names, e.g., *Shiva*. Calling Him *God* is like calling your friend *man* instead of their name. A *noun* is "a person, place, or thing"—not a proper name. In the King James Version of the Bible and most translations, the proper name of God cannot be found. Why could this be? The sons of God will know their Daddy's name and have it written in their hearts and on their foreheads. True sovereignty knows the proper name of God. If you have made it this far in this book you are blessed and highly favored. There can be no relationship if we do not know someone's name, we are privileged to have His names and faces revealed to us. *"Do not hurt the earth, the sea, or the trees till we have sealed the servants of our God on their foreheads,"* (Revelation 7:3). *"His servants shall serve Him. They shall see His face, and His name shall be on their foreheads,"* (Revelation 22:4).

PROPHETIC WORD

Jesus prophesied to Israel in (Matthew 23:39), "...*you shall see Me no more till you say, 'Blessed is He who comes in the name of the LORD [YOD HEY WAH HEY]*!" In this verse, Jesus predicted that Israel would be blinded for a season, but the time would come that would be marked by a sign—messengers coming in the name of " *YOD HEY WAH HEY.*" Many have come in the name of Jesus, but how many have come in the name of YHWH? Israel was and still is scattered across the face of the earth. When they hear the redemptive message of GOD's name, *"Behold the Hand, Behold the Nail,"* they will make the association with Jesus and declare, *"Blessed is He who comes in the name of Yod Hey Wah Hey."* Not only will they know that Jesus is their Messiah, but they will know He is the God of Creation. Then they will have one king over them, and we will see the kingdom of God ushered in; anything else is an illusion—a creation of man. Yes, when Jesus breaks through the clouds, there will be a company of sons standing on Mount Zion, *"… having His Father's name written on their foreheads"* (Revelation 14:1).

CHAPTER 13

SPIRITUAL WARFARE

"... For this purpose, the Son of God was manifested, that He might destroy the works of the devil."
(I John 3:8)

FOR TOO LONG THE church has been engaging in spiritual warfare out of its own resources and has been frustrated. We have been losing for too long. Effective spiritual warfare can only be waged with the anointing of the Holy Spirit. It's time believers get on solid ground from where they can obtain the victory! By releasing the power of the Holy Spirit through obedient warriors, the power centers of the Enemy are attacked and uprooted; through prophetic declarations Yahshua releases the blessing of His Kingdom in the earth. There are several keys in learning how to operate in spiritual warfare that are necessary for the spiritual warrior. A good Native warrior always made sure he has the finest weapons and good medicine before he engaged in battle. *"Let God arise, let His enemies be scattered ..."* (Psalm 68:1).

The centrality of the Holy Spirit In the scheme of obtaining victory in spiritual warfare cannot be over-emphasized; He is the key to victory. The Holy Spirit is the power center, the *dunamis*, or "the explosive dynamite power of God." The *dunamis* (Greek) contains the seed of YHWH, or His life-giving DNA. He is the source for empowering warriors to announce, advance, engage, reproduce and enforce the authority of YHWH, *"But you shall receive power* [dunamis] *when the Holy Spirit has come upon you ..."* (Acts 1:8).

Of course, the first key to victory in spiritual warfare is to have absolute confidence that we are on the winning side and in the foundational principles of Jesus' victory on the cross and in His resurrection. Revelation 19:10, *"...the testimony of Yahshua is the spirit of prophecy"*, should more accurately be interpreted: *"The martyrdom of Yahshua is the judicial decree that is shaping the destiny of the universe, and guiding the dynamics of history to complete YHWH's plan."* The word *testimony* in this verse should more accurately be interpreted as "martyrdom." We can be assured that God is guiding the dynamics of history to reflect His outcome. One of my pastors said, *"I know we are on the winning side because I read the end of the book!"*

The second key to victory in spiritual warfare is absolute assurance that Satan has been defeated, judged and cast out of heaven. In Ephesians chapter one, the believer is elevated to victorious heights in heavenly places through the resurrection of Yahshua. In the original Greek the phrase *"gave Him to be head"* (Ephesians 1"22) is the Greek word *calipha,* meaning *"He has seized the headship."* Yahshua has not only seized the headship but he pronounced judgment upon and decapitated His defeated foe.

> *"which He worked in Christ when He raised Him from the dead and seated Him at His right hand in the heavenly places, *[21]*far above all principality and power and might and dominion, and every name that is named, not only in this age but also in that which is to come, *[22]*And He put all things under His feet, and gave Him to be head over* [seized the headship] *all things to the church, *[23]*which is his body, the fullness of Him who f ills all in all"* (Ephesians 1:20-23).

Isaiah 2:2 gives us a glimpse at the dwelling place of the household of YHWH, *"Now it shall come to pass in the latter days that the mountain of the YHWH's house shall be established on the top of the mountains, and shall be exalted above the hills; and all nations shall flow to it."* Jesus reiterates this revelation in Matthew 16:18b, *"And on this rock (mountain) I will (okodome mou ecclacia) build a family of warriors, and the gates of hell shall not prevail against it!"* (My interpretation). First let us examine the phrase, *"the Gates of Hell"*.

Yahshua journeyed from Tyre and Sidon, where not much information is given, but we can deduce, in the prophetic dimension, that His trip there was high level spiritual warfare to deal with the Kings of Tyre and Sidon spoken of in Ezekiel 28. From there He journeyed back to the sea of Galilee where he dealt with high level spiritual strongholds on land and sea. From there he traveled north to the foot of Mount Hermon at Caesarea Philippi, where He made His famous proclamation *"On this rock I will build my church and the gates of hell will not prevail against it,"* (Matthew 16:17-19). This is an important location in understanding high level spiritual warfare and end time prophecy. After telling the disciples that the gates of hell will not prevail against them, they took a six days journey to the top of Mount Herman. From there Yahshua gave the disciples a Master's Degree education in visions and revelations in spiritual warfare.

Yahshua took the disciples to the summit of Mount Herman and there, *"He was transfigured before them, His face shone like the sun, and His clothes became white as light. And Moses and Eliyah appeared to them talking with Him,"* (Matthew 17:1-3). This was a high-level meeting on the top of the mountain. *"Suddenly a voice came out of heaven and said, 'this is My beloved Son, in whom I am well pleased, Hear Him!"* You listen to Him!!! Jesus began to teach them mysteries never revealed to mankind. From the top of Mount Herman Jesus prophetically declared war, *"And on this rock (mountain) I will (okodome mou ecclacia)*

build a family of warriors, and they will defeat the gates of hell!"
It was necessary for Him to reveal Himself in the glorified
state and to announce His Kingdom and ruling authority;
because in the future church age He would be presiding as
King of Kings from His glorified body. From this state He would
become the commander in chief of the armies of YHWH. He
nullified and reversed the works and demonic networks He had
observed during the temptation, when the Devil took Him
to the top of the same mountain. It was from the top of this
rock, Mount Herman, around 9232 ft that 200 fallen angels
descended and made covenant to release demons into the earth
to destroy humanity and topple YHWH's kingdom. It was from
here that the *"Gates of Hell"* were released. If you have seen the
logo of Paramount Studios, you have seen the 22 stars that
come out of heaven and circle a mountain. That my friends are a
picture of the 22 leaders of the fallen angels that descended from
heaven to the top of Mount Hermon and developed their
plans to destroy humanity. (All of this information can be
found in the Book of Enoch beginning at chapter six). The high-
level message Jesus was delivering to the disciples was that from
the top of this mountain (rock) His victorious army of Sons and
Daughters would defeat all of the gates of hell.

Yahshua descended the mountain and His first encounter
was a demon. This demon had been sent to challenge Yahshua's
newly proclaimed war plan. The child's father cried out for help
because Yahshua's disciples could not cast it out. Yahshua said, *"If
you have faith as a mustard seed, you will say **to this mountain**,
move from here to there it will move, and nothing will be impossible
to you. However, this kind does not go out except by prayer
and fasting."* (Matthew 17:20-21). The mountain He was
referring to here was not the demon possessed child, but he is
speaking prophetically of the gates of hell from Mount Herman.
It just takes a mustard seed of faith to access all of the powers
of the kingdom of YHWH and you can move mountains,
demonic strongholds. It was there that He spoke to the

mountain (the demonic stronghold over the child) and it was removed. YHWH's army of spiritual warriors will defeat the Gates of Hell.

Group prayer is wonderful, but, more often than not, you will find yourself alone—just you and the Holy Spirit. Several years ago, I was living in Bozeman, Montana, when I was confronted with a powerful stronghold of the Enemy. I happen to believe in the spiritual realm. I have no doubts of its reality and the existence of evil spirits and principalities and powers. I came home from work one night and was reading the local newspaper when I came across an advertisement for an abortion clinic. My spirit revolted! I felt sick to my stomach, but what I read next almost knocked me down. The address for the abortion clinic was only one block away from my house. The Holy Spirit arose up within me, and I declared, *"No way, this isn't happening on my watch!"* The first thought that came to my mind was to call my pastor to see if we could arrange a prayer meeting.

> The Holy Spirit quickly rebuked me and said, *"No! You go and pray now!"* I got up, put on my coat, and told my wife that I was going for a prayer walk. When I got to the clinic address, I said, *"Okay, Holy Spirit, what do I do now?"* Holy Spirit said, *"Walk around the block seven times proclaiming My kingdom."*

> I did as the Holy Spirit instructed. No one was there to watch me or hear me; it was just me and the Holy Spirit. After I finished the seventh round, I asked, *"What do I do now?"*

> The Holy Spirit said, *"Take authority over the baby-killing demon, cast out every spiritual stronghold and bind it to its judgment. Then proclaim the dominion of King Jesus over this place."*

Once again, I did as the Holy Spirit directed—not just for one night. For three months I walked around that place and proclaimed the kingdom because Jesus promised, "*...whatever things you ask when you pray, believe that you receive them, and you will have them*" (Mark 11:24). After the third month, I was reading the *Bozeman Chronicle*, and to my amazement, a news clip *apologized* for the closure of the abortion clinic! "Hallelujah! Is that just coincidence, or is it God?" I have many more experiences I could share, but these are just a few. Jesus said, "*... if I cast out devils by the Spirit of God, surely the kingdom of God has come ...*" (Matthew 12:28).

The lives of Native American warriors are a great illustration on preparation for spiritual warfare. The preparation of warriors was in body, soul, and spirit. The goal of the warrior was not only to perfect his individual combat skills but to obtain spiritual help that would make him invincible; this is more commonly known as "Indian medicine." Native American warriors such as Crazy Horse, Geronimo, and Crowfoot believed in their medicine so strongly that they were convinced their enemies could not kill them. Warriors would become so empowered, many of them believed they could not be killed in battle and would charge directly into the line of fire.

One story tells about a battle that ensued between the Blackfeet and the Crow, two mortal enemies who had come together to smoke the pipe to make peace. But this peace meeting was unknown to a party of Blackfeet warriors who were returning to camp from a hunting expedition, and they encountered two young Crow bucks. The boys were quickly captured and killed.

When word got out about the killing, the Crows gathered to retaliate. During the night, they attacked the Blackfeet encampment. The Blackfeet quickly responded and drove the Crows into a gully in a river bottom. From there, the Crow warriors were safely covered and could easily defend themselves, returning fire to the enemy surrounding them. The Blackfeet continued their attack throughout the night but could not penetrate the enemy lines.

Finally, the Blackfeet war chief halted the battle and consulted his compatriots. They realized that it was futile to continue their current strategy of encirclement without sacrificing many warriors. The war chief ordered the warriors to mount a single-line charge, with horse behind horse. The *Ee Doh Moh*, or warrior leader, took the lead and charged headlong into the direct fire of the entrenched enemy stronghold, leaping over their heads with his warriors charging right behind him. They easily broke through the enemy lines, effectively routing the Crow warriors.

Warriors like Crazy Horse, Crowfoot, Geronimo, Red Cloud, and many others who believed they could not be killed in battle had the stories of close encounters to prove their feats in battle. "...*When the enemy comes in like a flood, the Spirit of the Lord* [YHWH] *will lift up a standard against him*" (Isaiah 59:19).

From the time they were born, native warriors were trained, not as killers but with a mindset instilled to protect and guard their people. Hunting skills and virtues like wisdom, bravery, generosity, humility, and honesty were highly valued and modeled to the youth by their fathers and elders. Status in the camp was earned, and respect and honors were attained by young men who displayed those characteristics. The young boys grew up under the tutelage and mentoring of their fathers and men who had obtained the honor of being called *Ninna* (Father). When a youth arrived at a certain age, he was sent on a vision quest to seek spiritual powers; this was his "rite of passage." The vision quest consisted of at least three or four days of fasting in the wilderness, usually in a high place, until the youth encountered a spirit being who would become his spirit guide or medicine. The spirit guide would teach the youth his personal song and dance to be used to invoke empowerment.

The warrior invoked his powers *through fasting and purification* (this kind comes out by prayer and fasting) Purification would take place in the sweat lodge and with prayers, and smudging with sweetgrass or sage. The warrior would artfully put on his war paint and regalia, much like Paul instructed believers to put on the full armor of God. Drum songs would be sung during purification, and finally the warriors would dance the war dance. Warriors would dance until the spirit came upon them, and they were endued with power (this is also how believers receive anointing). The songs sung by Native Americans always contain the name *Hayah* or other forms of the name of God, which I believe are evidence of their relationship with the post-flood First Nations. Warriors danced until their medicine empowered them and protected them in battle. *"Finally, my brethren, be strong in the Lord and in the power of His might. ¹¹Put on the whole armor of God that you may be able to stand against the wiles of the devil"* (Ephesians 6:10, 11). Paul was letting us know there is a way of preparing for battle and I believe it is more than a little prayer. Jesus says it involves prayer and fasting.

These are just a few examples of the time Native American warriors spent in preparation for battle. Here, I need to emphasize, that as children of YHWH, we seek empowerment from the Holy Spirit and not any other entity. I believe that if Christians took spiritual warfare as seriously as Native warriors and got out of their pews and spent time in prayer and preparation of spirit, soul and body, we would see the tide turn in our favor. As I have already mentioned, the anointing comes from encountering Jesus, and we need to spend time and effort seeking His face. The closer you get to Jesus, the more anointing you will experience. The more anointing you experience, the more courage and confidence you will experience. The more confidence and anointing you gain, the more demons you will drive out. The more anointing you carry in your ministry, the more edification to the body of Christ. The more edification to the Body of Christ the more His kingdom is advanced, *"And from the days of John the Baptist until now the Kingdom of heaven suffers violence, and the violent take it by force,"* (Matthew 11:12).

The church has been practicing spiritual warfare on a lower level, and individual believers need to find deliverance in their personal lives. Instead of preaching deliverance from sin and flesh modern-day preachers leave their congregations living in a fleshly religious existence. How many preachers have you heard repeating the lie, *"We are all sinners saved by grace"?* We are not sinners; believers need to be delivered from the works of the flesh and from the realm of sin and death. Believers need to be set free of societal bondages, poverty, generational curses, and a worldly mindset of unbelief. It's time to elevate our level of warfare and enter into a higher spiritual walk of sonship and kingdom authority. Spiritual warfare should be a daily activity. *"For the law of the Spirit of life in Christ Jesus has made me free from the law of sin and death. For what the law could not do in that it was weak through the flesh, God did ..."* (Romans 8:2, 3).

Through the years I learned the power of group prayer—especially when the group knows how to operate in spiritual warfare. Jesus said,*"... that if two of you agree on earth concerning anything they ask, it will be done for them by My Father in heaven"* (Matthew 18:19). One experience that stands out took place in Glasgow, Montana, where a small group of us were gathering weekly for prayer. One evening someone asked what we should pray for. A popular local bar had become notorious for rugged parties, bar fights and drug dealing, so we agreed to ask God to shut it down. Over the weekend, God not only shut it down, He burned it to the ground! We all looked at each other and said, "Coincidence or God?" Since that time, I have seen many such answered prayers, and I cannot doubt the power of God and praying saints.

Throughout the years of actively participating in spiritual warfare I have been involved with intercessors and intercessory prayer. For some reason God always put me together with them. My problem was not with them but with myself. My style of prayer always seemed to be more militant and aggressive while their style of prayer seemed to be more emotional and feeling the burdens in the spirit. The Holy Spirit reconciled this confusion for me out of the Book of Enoch. God's angel took Enoch by the spirit to the mountain of God. Around the mountain on all sides were multitudes kneeling and making intercession. Enoch asked the angel who these people were and he said these are intercessors. Enoch asked, who are these on the north side of the mountain and the angel replied, these are worshippers who make intercession for God's people. Those on the east side made intercession for believers around the world who were being persecuted and martyred. The ones on the south also made intercession but my attention was drawn to the ones on the west side. Enoch inquired about these people and the angel replied, these are warrior intercessors, they are the ones who make war with the enemy. Hallelujah! That pulled it all together for me; I realized that I am a part of the intercessory ministry but my role is that of a warrior. My Indian name is Ee Doh Moh. This is an honorable name and refers to a war chief or a leader of warriors; for instance, he is the one who leads the warriors into battle. My name was given to me by a tribal elder who received it from the Holy Spirit. Indian names are not just words but are descriptions of a person's nature.

CHAPTER 14

"THE SIGN OF THE SON OF MAN"

"Now I saw the heavens opened and behold a white horse.
And He who sat upon him was called Faithful and True, And in
righteousness He judges and makes war.
His eyes were like a flame of fire, and on His head
Were many crowns. He had a name written
That no one knew except He Himself.
He was clothed with a robe dipped in blood,
And His name is called the Word of God".
Revelation (19:11-13)

IN MATTHEW TWENTY-FOUR THE disciples asked Jesus, *"When will these things be, what will be the sign of your coming, and the end of the age."* I'm looking forward to seeing Him face to face. It won't be long and we will see Him. I believe that most of YHWH's children are sensing that we are nearing the time of His coming. All signs prophesied in the word of God are beginning to line up and world events are unfolding right before our eyes. Many Biblical time lines are coming to their conclusion, such as "Daniels seventy weeks," "the Seven One Thousand Years Calendar," and the "Shemita cycles, and more." I am not addressing these timelines; but, in this chapter, we are going to disclose the "Sign of the Son of Man".

The book of Revelation is the revealing or unveiling of Yashua Ha Mashiach, Jesus Christ. Chapter nineteen gives a picture of our victorious soon coming warrior King, the Mashiach (Messiah), sitting on a white horse and crowned with many crowns. A prophetic friend of mine had a powerful vision one night during a conference; in the vision He saw Jesus, sitting on a white horse, dressed in the regalia of a Blackfeet warrior. Blackfeet regalia is distinct from other tribes in the headdress with the eagle feathers pointing straight up, like a stove pipe. As he approached Jesus, he asked Him, *"Why are you wearing the headdress of a Blackfeet warrior?"* Messiah answered, *'I wear the crown of every nation."* The White Horse prophetically is EliYah, the Holy Spirit, who carries Jesus into the battle. The crowns do not represent every country in the world, but the crowns of the nations that God intended from the foundation of the world, Matthew 25:32, *"All the nations will be gathered before Him and He will separate them one from another, ... Then the King will say to those on His right hand, 'come you blessed of My Father, inherit the kingdom prepared for you from the foundation of the world ... Then He will say to those on His left hand, depart from Me you cursed, into the everlasting fire prepared for the Devil and his angels."* (Notice the emphasis on, nations prepared from the foundation of the world). God had a plan before the world began and He is completing His purposes. Wow, this verse illuminated me, knowing His will challenges us to come into alignment with His plans and purposes. He had a plan from before the foundation of the World and it has never changed. He is going to complete His plans and purposes until they will be completed in seven days, (According to the "Year is a thousand days calendar"). The Millennial reign of Jesus will complete the seven thousand years.

Chapter nineteen says, *"He had a name written that no one knew except He Himself. He was clothed with a robe dipped in blood, and His name is called the Word of God."* Revelation (19:11-13). He clearly says, He has a name written that no one knows but then He says His name is called the Word of God. It is an oxymoron because even when it is clearly written before men's eyes, they still don't get it, that is why it's a being revealed to the Sons of YHWH. To understand we must look into the language that Jesus was speaking to the Apostle John. In Revelation 1:8 and 11, 21:6, 22:13, Jesus declares His name *"Aleph/Tau"*, our versions say, "Alpha and Omega. Our Bibles were translated from Greek into English but the language that Jesus was speaking was the original language of creation, the Paleo Hebrew. The Alpha and Omega are the first and last letters of the Greek alphabet but Jesus would have spoken in the Hebrew *Aleph Beht.* The name written upon His thigh that no man knows but He Himself is *Aleph/Tav,* the first and last letters in the Hebrew Aleph Beht. If Jesus says He is Aleph/Tav then He is Aleph/Tav, no arguments. Jesus is *Aleph/Tav!* The *Aleph/Tav* is the Word of God, for by them Elohim created the heavens and the earth.

Most people don't get it. A few years ago, I was hiking in the mountains with my kids and we came to a very ominous high cliff. My kids crawled on top of it and began shouting, *"I am the king of the world."* We all laughed and didn't pay any attention to their little declaration. That is how most of us read the bible, we just rush through and miss a lot of valuable revelation.

את

A couple of years ago the Holy Spirit led me to study Psalm 119. In it I discovered that each of the 22 sections are headed by a Hebrew letter and the corresponding pictograph of the 22 original Hebrew letters. This prompted me to study each Hebrew letter, wow, this opened up a whole new world of revelation to me that I had never imagined. For instance, the seventh letter is the Zayin; the seventh position in the

Aleph Beht is a very prominent position because seven is the number of God's ordinal perfection and completion. The pictograph represents a weapon or a sword, through which He is telling us we are going to have to fight in order to get the victory, put on the full armor of God and take the sword of the Spirit, which is the word of God. This is a time of spiritual warfare in the heavenly realms and the world is a reflection of what is happening in the heavenlies. We must take up our weapons to complete His plans and purposes.

The plan of Satan has been to hide and obscure the full revelation of YHWH; for instance, God's name the Tetragrammaton, YHWH, has been hidden, but also the Aleph/Tav has been hidden. The Tetragrammaton was taken out of the Bible over 6700 times and replaced with the word LORD. The Aleph/Tav has been taken out of the bible over 10,600 times, according to the Strong's Concordance, and is interpreted as "et, and". Isn't that amazing? The first question most believers ask is, *"Why would they take the names out of the Bible and who would do that?"* Our Bibles have been tampered with just enough to keep believers from attaining God's perfection. The ultimate deceiver is the master deceiver himself, Satan who has tampered with scripture. Nevertheless, we are living in the day that YHWH God is restoring His full revelation. With the discovery of the Dead Sea Scrolls and the restoration of the Paleo Aleph Beht, we are recovering much truth that was lost or covered up. Jesus warned His followers to beware of the leaven of the Pharisees and Sadducees. The leaven being deception through our own scriptures.

Here is some of my favorite verses in Torah where Aleph/Tav is used, *"In the beginning God created the heavens and the earth."* The original language reads, *"In the beginning created God Aleph/Tav, the heavens, Aleph/Tav, the earth."* The original language reveals to us that Elohim is Aleph/Tav. Another great verse is Isaiah 6:1 *"In the year that King Uzziah died, I saw the Lord sitting on a throne, high and lifted up."* The original language says, *"In the year died King Uzziah, I saw Aleph/Tav Adonai sitting on a throne."* In the book of Malachi 4:5 *"Behold I will send you Elijah the prophet,"* in the original Paleo text it reads, *"Behold, I will send you Aleph/Tav Elijah the prophet."* Also, in Joel 2:28, *"I will pour out my Spirit upon all flesh,"* and in the original Paleo, *"I will pour out Aleph/Tav my Spirit."* Maybe the scribes and interpreters didn't know Aleph/Tav and just left it out but, nevertheless, it was a grievous error. Many references do not recognize the Aleph/Tav so you have to learn how to recognize the Hebrew pictographs yourself in the original language to find the references, but Aleph/Tav is laced throughout the Torah. It is beautiful when you receive and understand.

The Paleo Hebrew Aleph is depicted as an ox head and the description of the pictograph is that of a strong leader or the head man, strong, humble. It also symbolizes God the Father.

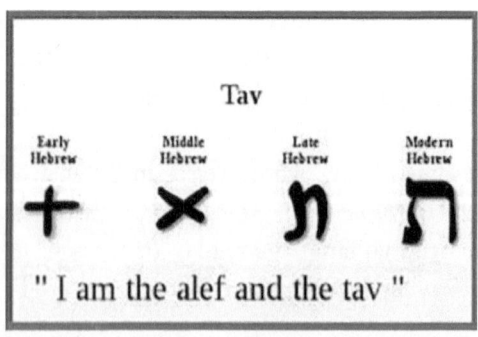

The Paleo letter Tav is depicted as a cross or an X and the description of the pictograph is a covenant, a sign or signature; the Tav is the 22nd letter of the Aleph Beht and is the last or the end. Tav literally means a mark. The ancient letter was in the form of an X or cross. Even today, someone who is illiterate signs their "mark" with an X … The Aleph/Tau represents the whole word of God, by which the worlds were created. **The Hebrew Aleph/Tav** symbol is a deeply meaningful word and is found in all the original texts of the Bible. It is the first and last letters of the Hebrew alphabet.

Why is all of this important and what does it have to do with the end times? I believe the Aleph/Tav is not only Jesus's name but it is also His signature written on His thigh. I entitled this chapter, **"The Sign of the Son of Man,"** because the world is on the verge of the sign of the Son of man appearing in the heavens.

> *"Immediately after the tribulation of those days the sun will be darkened, and the moon will not give its light; the stars will fall from heaven, and the powers of the heavens will be shaken. **Then the sign of the Son of Man will appear in heaven**, and then all of the tribes of the earth shall mourn, and they will see the Son of Man coming on the clouds of heaven with power and great glory, and He will send His angels with the great sound of a trumpet, and they will gather together His elect from the four winds, from one end of heaven to the other."*
> (Matthew 24:29-31)

I am not predicting a date but I am letting the word of God speak for itself and you can draw the conclusions you believe is right. This sign will all occur on April 8, 2024 with the appearance of the Sign of the Son of Man in the heavens. The date is set by the eclipse of the sun that will take place on April 8th, 2024 during Passover season. Jesus said in Matthew 24, the sun will be darkened and the moon will not give its light; this phenomenon can only happen during an eclipse of the sun when the moon passes between the earth and the sun and all light is blocked out, the sun is darkened and the moon does not give its light. During this eclipse the stars will fall from heaven and the powers of the heavens will be shaken; the stars are the power structures the ruling principalities and powers set up by Satan will be shaken and cast down. I believe this is a revelation that the world needs to know and I am releasing this word while there is still time. Many end time eschatologists pointed to the Revelation Chapter twelve sign of the Woman clothed with the Sun as the sign of the Son of Man. In 2017 there was an astrological alignment in the heavens where the birth of the man child appeared in the womb of the constellation of Virgo. Prophets jumped on the band wagon and began to say this was the sign of the Son of Man. The only problem with that sign is that all of the trigger points have already passed.

In Genesis chapter one verse fourteen God created the Sun and the moon and He said, "*Let them be for signs and seasons and for night, and for day.*" God will use these eclipses His sign and signature, an eclipse falls within that definition. When the Aleph/Tav appears, we know that it is the signature of Jesus. This sign began in 2017 when a great eclipse appeared over the USA and passed from Salem Oregon across the continent and exited at Salem South Carolina. The second eclipsed just recently occurred on October 14, 2023 and passed from the Oregon coast and exited on the Texas coast. There will be a third eclipse April 8th, 2024; this eclipse will pass from Texas and intersect the eclipse of 2023 in Texas and the eclipse of 2017 in Cairo Illinois. The paths of the three eclipses over America will form a perfect Aleph/Tav. This cannot be made up. It will happen and cannot be denied. It is the signature of the Son of Man in the heavens!

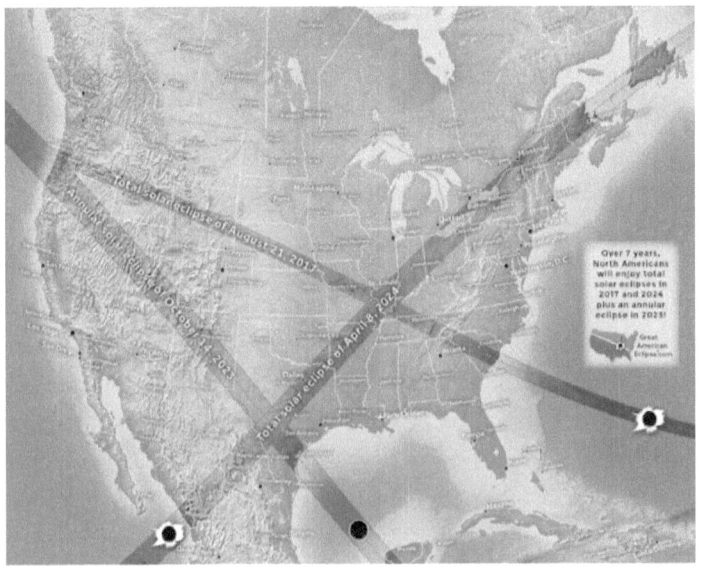

(Credit Map by NASA)

The Aleph is clearly visible in this NASA illustration and a double Tav is formed at the intersections of the eclipses emphasizing the end. Jesus said, *"I am Aleph/Tav, the first and the last, the beginning and the end, the Almighty."* He also said, *"When you see the sign of the Son of Man appear in heaven … He will gather together His elect from the four winds of heaven."* Why would the signature of Jesus appear at this time, and why would it appear over the USA? Allow me to speculate.

I believe that the appearance of the sign of the Son of Man marks the end of the age, as the disciples asked, *"What will be the sign of your coming and the end of the age?"* The end of the world is the end of the age the six thousand years allotted for mankind to rule on the earth. It will mark the end of Satan's reign of terror with the stars falling from heaven. The bible says, *Babylon has fallen*; all of the false power structures in the world will lose their power and the time of their judgment has arrived. The United States will stand in the Matthew 25 judgment of nations and it is my conclusion that it will stand with all other nations that have illegally usurped sovereign authority and established governments outside of God. Those will stand on the left hand of Jesus and all First Nations and Nations of God will stand on His right hand and inherit the kingdoms prepared for them from before the foundation of the world. All authority imparted to God ordained nations will be reinstated and their ruling jurisdiction will be resumed, as they make Jesus their king.

It is a common mistake to equate The Great Tribulation with the Wrath of God. Modern eschatologists have created doctrines called the Great Tribulation that is not in the word of God. Yes, we are in a time of great tribulation, and tribulation has been here since at least 2017. Clearly, we can discern that the Four Horsman of the Apocalypse have already been released. The world has entered into a time of refinement and judgment and a remnant will emerge out of the Seal Judgments. It is a time of separation, of refinement, and purification. During this time the five wise and five foolish virgins will appear, the sons of the kingdom will mature and it is possible the great falling away has occurred. This sets the stage for the Anti-Christ to appear and for the Wrath of YHWH to be poured out. Saints we are closer to the return of Jesus than we have been led to believe. But one thing we can be assured of, God's children will not be left for the wrath of YHWH!

The central theme of Come into my Father's Teepee is for the children of God to return to their place in the presence of YHWH. He is the most loving and the most beautiful being in and through and above all. It would take volumes of books to write all YHWH has for us for this time, but it is my prayer that you have received this message as word from EliYah, the Holy Spirit. I have endeavored to lay out the Word of God as simply and as accurately as I am able. It has taken me years to understand truths about the kingdom of God and the revelation of *the family of God,* and I believe these are being revealed to others around the world. In this hour believers are receiving YHWH God's invitation to come into His teepee *and become His family.* This is the time of the awakening of the sons of God and the ingathering of the family of YHWH, "*...He will baptize you with the Holy Spirit and fire. ¹²His winnowing fork is in His hand, and He will thoroughly clear His threshing floor; and He will gather His wheat into the barn; but He will burn up the chaff with unquenchable fire*" (Matthew 3:11, 12, NASB).

The revelation of God's family and the exposing of Mystery Babylon will cause a great separation between the sons of God and the established religious order. Jesus said, "*They will put you out of their synagogues, yes, the time is coming that whoever kills you will think that he offers God service. ³And these things they will do to you because they have not known the Father ...*" (John 16:2, 3). This verse points to the fact that many religious folks do not know YHWH, and not everyone will receive His message. The separation of the sons of God from the church will be through much pain and heartache. It's time to leave Babylon. Jesus said, those who follow Him through the troubled waters and remain "*...are called, chosen, and faithful*", (Revelation 17:14).

As a Native American evangelist and a man of God, I am anticipating the run down the home stretch. The message is clear, the goal is in sight, and I am excited. I count it all joy to know that His name is being written on the tables of my heart and in my mind. My prayer every night before I drift off into dreamland is: "*Father, write Your name on the tables of my heart and in my mind, that when You come You will find me with Your name written upon me.*" This is an important point, Jesus is coming for those who have His Father's name written on them; Revelation 22:4, 3:12, 7:3, 14:1. Blessings to you all and hope to see you, *in my Father's Teepee.* For those wishing further consultation please feel free to contact me, (*lockleybremner@gmailcom*).

SOURCES CONSULTED

"Babylon the Harlot." www/discoverrevelation.com/9.html, accessed 1 June 2016.

Bierce, Ambrose. 1885.

Braun, T. T.

Bremner, Lockley. *The Original People's Bible,* 2004.

Corey, Benjamin L. "10 Reasons Why People Leave Church." 7 August 2013, *Patheos: Hosting the Conversation on Faith,* http://www.patheos.com/blogs/formerlyfundie/10-reasons-why-people-leave-church/, accessed 18 June 2016.

Clark, Dr. F. Stoner. "Is Church Renewal a Viable Option?" *His Presence on Line: Preparing the Church for the Second Coming of Christ.* 8 March 2015. http://hispresenceonline. org/the-end-times/church-renewal-pipe-dream-or- viable-option-2/, accessed 16 June 2016.

Collins, Steven. "The United States of America in Biblical Prophecy."2009.stevenmcollins.com/html/usa_in_prophecy. html, accessed 18 June 2016.

Culp-Pressler, Tara. "The Shocking Rates of Violence and Abuse Facing Native American Kids. 18 November, 2014. http://thinkprogress.org/health/2014/11/18/3593300/violence-native-american-kids/, accessed 17 June 2016.

Dempsey, Hugh A."Dictionary of Canadian Biography."1982. http://www.biographi.ca/en/bio/isapo_muxika_11E. html, accessed 17 June 2016.

Dictionary.com.

Dietz, Frank. "Twenty-Eight Principles that Helped Build America." 15 April 2016. https://twitter.com/frankdietz/status/720941769689423872, accessed 17 June 2016.

Elwell, Douglas. *Planet X, The Sign of the Son of Man and the End of the Age.* Crane, Mo: Defender Publishing, 2010.

Grinnell, George Bird. "Native American Legends, Blackfoot Legends–First Medicine Lodge," 1913, www.legendsofamerica.com/na-medicinelodge.html, accessed 17 June, 2016.

"Hebrew Word Studies." www.logosapostolic.org, accessed 17 June 2016.

Lane, Bo. "Why Do So Many Pastors Leave the Ministry? The Facts Will Shock You." *Expastors.com.* 2012-2015. http://www.expastors.com/why-do-so-many-pastors-leave-the-ministry-the-facts-will-shock-you/, accessed 17 June 2016.

Marcus. "Servant King." info@servantking.info.

Owings, Alison. *Indian Voices: Listening to Native Americans.* New Brunswick, NJ: Rutgers University Press, 2001.

Penington, Isaac. *Writings from the Kingdom of God.*

"Police Dynamics: Power for Effective Law Enforcement." 25 March 2011. https://policedynamics.wordpress.com/2011/03/05/gov, accessed 17 June 2016.

Scherman, Rabbi Nosson. *Tanach the Stone edition*. XXV. Brooklyn: Mesorah Publications, Ltd., 1996.

Smith, Herschel. "The Captain's Journal: Bureau of Land Management Versus Cliven Bundy." 13 April 2014, *The Captain's Journal*, http://www.captainsjournal. com/2014/04/13/bureau-of-land-management-versus-cliven-bundy-post-mortem/, accessed 17 June 2016.

"Sovereignty."10 June 2016. https://en.wikipedia.org/wiki/sovereignty, accessed 18 June 2016.

Spier, Leslie. *The Prophet Dance of the Northwest and Its Derivatives: The Source of the Ghost Dance*. Menasha, Wis.: George Banta Publishing Co, 1935.

Sproul, R. C. "What Does *coram Deo* Mean?" *Ligonier Ministries*. 27 May 2015. www.ligonier.org/blog/*what-does-coram-deo-mean*/, accessed 18 June 2016.

"Statistics in the Ministry." *Pastoral Care, Inc.*. 2016. http://www.pastoralcareinc.com/statistics, accessed 18 June 2016.

Stockstill, Larry. *The Remnant: Restoring Integrity to American Ministry*. Lake Mary, Fla.: Charisma House, 2008.

Strong, James, LLD., S.T.D. *The New Strong's Exhaustive Concordance of the Bible*. Thomas Nelson Publishers, 1984

Wikipedia.com.

NASA (gov): *Great American Eclipse*. https://www, greatamericaneclipse.com